THE HANDY SCIENCE ANSWER BOOK™

Second Edition

Compiled by the Science and Technology Department
of the Carnegie Library of Pittsburgh

VISIBLE
INK
PRESS

DETROIT

THE HANDY SCIENCE
ANSWER BOOK™
Second Edition

Published by Visible Ink Press™
a division of The Gale Group
27500 Drake Road
Farmington Hills, MI 48331-3535

Visible Ink Press is a trademark of The Gale Group

Most Visible Ink Press™ books are available at special quantity discounts when purchased in bulk by corporations, organizations, or groups. Customized printings, special imprints, messages, and excerpts can be produced to meet your needs. For more information, contact Special Markets Manager, Visible Ink Press, 27500 Drake Road, Farmington Hills, MI 48331. Or call 1-800-347-4253.

Art Director: Mary Krzewinski
Typesetter: Marco Di Vita, Graphix Group

ISBN 1-57859-112-0

Contents

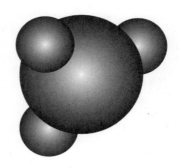

SPACE

EARTH

ENVIRONMENT

BIOLOGY

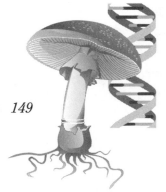

COMMUNICATIONS

Credits

Line art illustrations by Hans & Cassady of Westerville, Ohio.

Photographs of nine-banded armadillo, monarch butterfly, sundew, and Grand Canyon National Park provided by Robert J. Huffman/Field Mark Publications. Additional photographs provided by the Library of Congress, the National Aeronautics and Space Administration, the National Park Service, the U.S. Department of Agriculture, and the U.S. Fish and Wildlife Service.

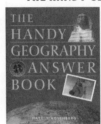
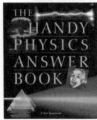
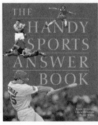

PHYSICS AND CHEMISTRY

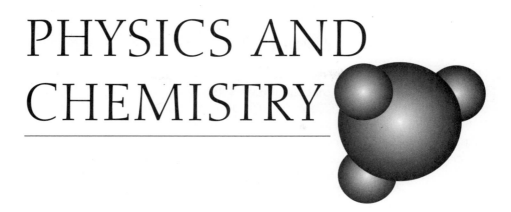

ENERGY, MOTION, FORCE, AND HEAT

See also: Energy

How is **"absolute zero"** defined?

Absolute zero is the theoretical temperature at which all substances have zero thermal energy. Originally conceived as the temperature at which an ideal gas at constant pressure would contract to zero volume, absolute zero is of great significance in thermodynamics and is used as the fixed point for absolute temperature scales. Absolute zero is equivalent to 0°K, -459.67°F, or -273.15°C.

The velocity of a substance's molecules determines its temperature; the faster the molecules move, the more volume they require, and the higher the temperature becomes. The lowest actual temperature ever reached was two-billionth of a degree above absolute zero (2×10^{-9}K) by a team at the Low Temperature Laboratory in the Helsinki University of Technology, Finland, in October, 1989.

Does **hot water freeze faster** than cold?

A bucket of hot water will not freeze faster than a bucket of cold water. However, a bucket of water that *has been* heated or boiled, then allowed to cool to the same temperature as the bucket of cold water, may freeze faster. Heating or boiling drives out some of the air bubbles in water; because air bubbles cut down thermal conductivity, they can inhibit freezing. For the same reason, previously heated water forms denser ice than unheated water, which is why hot-water pipes tend to burst before cold-water pipes.

1

What is **superconductivity**?

Superconductivity is a condition in which many metals, alloys, organic compounds, and ceramics conduct electricity without resistance, usually at low temperatures. Heinke Kamerlingh Omnes, a Dutch physicist, discovered superconductivity in 1911, but it was not until 1972 that the modern theory regarding the phenomenon was developed by three American physicists—John Bardeen, Leon N. Cooper, and John Robert Schrieffer. Known as the *BCS theory* after the three scientists, it postulates that superconductivity occurs in certain materials because the electrons in them, rather than remaining free to collide with imperfections and scatter, form pairs that can flow easily around imperfections and do not lose their energy. A variety of uses have been proposed for this phenomenon, including switching devices that control electronic circuits in computers; devices that measure extremely small magnetic fields for medical diagnosis; and the means to develop powerful superconducting magnets used to build particle accelerators.

What is **inertia**?

Inertia is a tendency of all objects and matter in the universe to stay still, or if moving, to continue moving in the same direction, unless acted on by some outside force. This forms the first law of motion formulated by Isaac Newton (1642–1727). To move a body at rest, enough external force must be used to overcome the object's inertia; the larger the object is, the more force is required to move it. In his *Philosophae Naturalis Principia Mathematica*, published in 1687, Newton sets forth all three laws of motion. Newton's second law is that the force to move a body is equal to its mass times its acceleration ($F = MA$), and the third law states that for every action there is an equal and opposite reaction.

Isaac Newton.

Why do **golf balls** have dimples?

The dimples minimize the drag (a force that makes a body lose energy as it moves through a fluid), allowing the ball to travel further than a smooth ball would. The air, as it passes a dimpled ball, tends to cling to the ball longer, reducing the eddies or wake effect that drain the ball's energy. The dimpled ball can travel up to 300 yards

Why does a boomerang return to its thrower?

Two well-known scientific principles dictate the characteristic flight of a boomerang: (1) the force of lift on a curved surface caused by air flowing over it; and (2) the unwillingness of a spinning gyroscope to move from its position.

When a person throws a boomerang properly, he or she causes it to spin vertically. As a result, the boomerang will generate lift, but it will be to one side rather than upwards. As the boomerang spins vertically and moves forward, air flows faster over the top arm at a particular moment than over the bottom arm. Accordingly, the top arm produces more lift than the bottom arm and the boomerang tries to twist itself, but because it is spinning fast, it acts like a gyroscope and turns to the side in an arc. If the boomerang stays in the air long enough, it will turn a full circle and return to the thrower. Every boomerang has a built-in orbit diameter, which is not affected by a person throwing the boomerang harder or spinning it faster.

(275 meters), but a smooth ball only goes 70 yards (65 meters). A ball can have 300 to 500 dimples that can be 0.01 inch (0.25 millimeter) deep. Another effect to get distance is to give the ball a backspin. With a backspin there is less air pressure on the top of the ball, so the ball stays aloft longer (much like an airplane).

What is **Maxwell's demon**?

An imaginary creature who, by opening and shutting a tiny door between two volumes of gases, could, in principle, concentrate slower molecules in one (making it colder) and faster molecules in the other (making it hotter), thus breaking the second law of thermodynamics. Essentially this law states that heat does not naturally flow from a colder body to a hotter body; work must be expended to make it do so. This hypothesis was formulated in 1871 by James C. Maxwell (1831–1879), who is considered to be the greatest theoretical physicist of the 19th century. The demon would bring about an effective flow of molecular kinetic energy. This excess energy would be useful to perform work and the system would be a perpetual motion machine. About 1950, the French physicist Léon Brillouin disproved Maxwell's hypothesis by demonstrating that the decrease in entropy resulting from the demon's actions would be exceeded by the increase in entropy in choosing between the fast and slow molecules.

Who is the founder of the science of **magnetism**?

The English scientist William Gilbert (1544–1603) regarded the Earth as a giant magnet, and investigated its magnetic field terms of dip and variation. He explored many other magnetic and electrostatic phenomena. The Gilbert (symbol Gb), a unit of magnetism, is named for him.

William Gilbert.

John H. Van Vleck (1899–1980), an American physicist, made significant contributions to modern magnetic theory. He explained the magnetic, electrical, and optical properties of many elements and compounds with the ligand field theory, demonstrated the effect of temperature on paramagnetic materials (called Van Vleck paramagnetism), and developed a theory on the magnetic properties of atoms and their components.

When was **spontaneous combustion** first recognized?

Spontaneous combustion is the ignition of materials stored in bulk. This is due to internal heat build-up caused by oxidation (generally a reaction in which electrons are lost, specifically when oxygen is combined with a substance, or when hydrogen is removed from a compound). Because this oxidation heat cannot be dissipated into the surrounding air, the temperature of the material rises until the material reaches its ignition point and bursts into flame.

A Chinese text written before 290 C.E. recognized this phenomenon in a description of the ignition of stored oiled cloth. The first Western recognition of spontaneous combustion was by J. P. F. Duhamel in 1757, when he discussed the gigantic conflagration of a stack of oil-soaked canvas sails drying in the July sun. Before spontaneous combustion was recognized, such events were usually blamed on arsonists.

What is **phlogiston**?

Phlogiston was a name used in the 18th century to identify a supposed substance given off during the process of combustion. The phlogiston theory was developed in the early 1700s by the German chemist and physicist, Georg Ernst Stahl (1660–1734).

In essence, Stahl held that combustible material such as coal or wood was rich in a material substance called "phlogiston." What remained after combustion was without phlogiston and could no longer burn. The rusting of metals also involved a transfer of phlogiston. This accepted theory explained a great deal previously unknown to chemists. For instance, metal smelting was consistent with the phlogiston theory. Charcoal in burning lost weight. Thus the loss of phlogiston either decreased or increased weight.

The French chemist Antoine Laurent Lavoisier (1743–1794) demonstrated that the gain of weight when a metal turned to a calx was just equal to the loss of weight of the air in the vessel. Lavoisier also showed that part of the air (oxygen) was indispensable to combustion, and that no material would burn in the absence of oxygen. The transition from Stahl's phlogiston theory to Lavoisier's oxygen theory marks the birth of modern chemistry at the end of the 18th century.

What is the **kindling point** of **paper**?

Paper ignites at 450°F (230°C).

What is an **adiabatic process**?

It is any thermodynamic process in which no heat transfer takes place between a system and its surrounding environment.

Does **water running down a drain** rotate in a different direction in the Northern and Southern Hemispheres?

If water runs out from a perfectly symmetrical bathtub, basin, or toilet bowl, in the Northern Hemisphere it would swirl counterclockwise; in the Southern Hemisphere, the water would run out clockwise. This is due to the Coriolis effect (the Earth's rotation influencing any moving body of air or water). However, some scientists think that the effect does not work on small bodies of water. Exactly on the equator, the water would run straight down.

What is a **Leyden jar**?

A Leyden jar, the earliest form of capacitor, is a device for storing an electrical charge. First described in 1745 by E. Georg van Kleist (c.1700–1748), it was also used by Pieter van Musschenbroek (1692–1761), a professor of physics at the University of Leyden. The device came to be known as a Leyden jar and was the first device that could store large amounts of electric charge. The jars contained an inner wire electrode in contact with water, mercury, or wire. The outer electrode was a human hand holding the jar. An improved version coated the jar inside and outside with separate metal foils with the inner foil connected to a conducting rod and terminated in a conducting sphere. This eliminated the need for the liquid electrolyte. In use, the jar was normally charged from an electrostatic generator. The Leyden jar is still used for classroom demonstrations of static electricity.

LIGHT, SOUND, AND OTHER WAVES

What is the **speed of light**?

The figure is 186,282 miles (299,792 kilometers) per second.

What are the **primary colors** in light?

Color is determined by the wavelength of its light (the distance between one crest of the light wave and the next). Those colors that blend to form "white light" are from shortest wave length to longest: red, orange, yellow, green, blue, indigo, and violet. All these monochromatic colors, except indigo, occupy large areas of the spectrum (entire range of wavelengths produced when a beam of electromagnetic radiation is broken up). These colors can be seen when a light beam is refracted through a prism. Some consider the primary colors to be six monochromatic colors that occupy large areas of the spectrum: red, orange, yellow, green, blue, and violet. Many physicists recognize three primary colors: red, yellow, and blue; or red, green, and blue, or red, green, and violet. All other colors can be made from these by adding two primary colors in various proportions. Within the spectrum, scientists have discovered 55 distinct hues. Infra-red and ultraviolet rays at each end of the spectrum are invisible to the human eye.

Why does the color of clothing appear different in sunlight than it does in a store under **fluorescent light**?

White light is a blend of all the colors, and each color has a different wavelength. Although sunlight and fluorescent light both appear as "white light," they each contain slightly different mixtures of these varying wavelengths. When sunlight and fluorescent light (white light) are absorbed by a piece of clothing, only some of the wavelengths (composing white light) reflect from the clothing. When the retina of the eye perceives the "color" of the clothing, it is really perceiving these reflected wavelengths. The mixture of wavelengths determines the color perceived. This is why an article of clothing sometimes appears to be a different color in the store than it does on the street.

What were **Anders Ångström's** contributions to the development of **spectroscopy**?

Swedish physicist and astronomer Anders Jonas Ångström (1814–1874) was one of the founders of spectroscopy. His early work provided the foundation for spectrum analysis (analysis of the ranges of electromagnetic radiation emitted or absorbed). He investigated the sun spectra as well as that of the Aurora Borealis. In 1868, he established measurements for wavelengths of greater than 100 Frauenhofer. In 1907, the angstrom (Å, equal to 10^{-10}m), a unit of wavelength measurement, was officially adopted.

Why was the **Michelson-Morley** experiment important?

This experiment on light waves, first carried out in 1881 by physicists Albert A. Michelson (1852–1931) and E. W. Morley (1838–1923) in the United States, is one of the historically significant experiments in physics and led to the development of Einsteins's theory of relativity. The original experiment, using the Michelson interferometer, attempted to detect the velocity of the Earth with respect to the hypothetical "luminiferous ether," a medium in space proposed to carry light waves. The procedure measured the speed of light in the direction of the Earth and the speed of light at right angles to the Earth's motion. No difference was found. This result discredited the ether theory and ultimately led to the proposal by Albert Einstein (1879–1955) that the speed of light is a universal constant.

Why does a **double sonic boom** occur when the space shuttle enters the atmosphere?

As long as an airborne object, such as a plane, is moving below the speed of sound (called Mach 1), the disturbed air remains well in front of the craft. But as the craft passes Mach 1 and is flying at supersonic speeds, a sharp air pressure rise occurs in front of the craft. In a sense the air molecules are crowded together and collectively impact. What is heard is a claplike thunder called a sonic boom or a supersonic bang. There are many shocks coming from a supersonic aircraft but these shocks usually combine to form two main shocks, one coming from the nose and one from the aft end of the aircraft. Each of the shocks moves at different velocities. If the time difference between the two shock waves is greater than 0.10 seconds apart, two sonic booms will be heard. This usually occurs when the aircraft ascends quickly. If the aircraft ascends more slowly, the two booms will sound like only one boom to the observer.

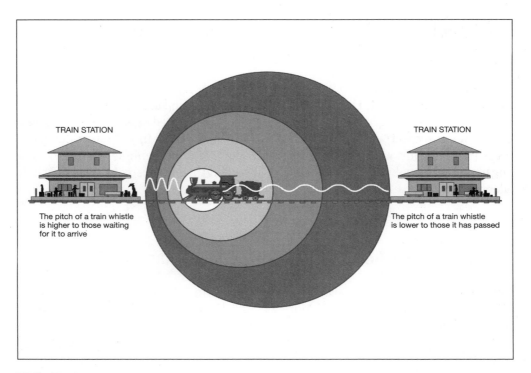

The pitch of a train whistle is higher to those waiting for it to arrive

TRAIN STATION

TRAIN STATION

The pitch of a train whistle is lower to those it has passed

The Doppler effect.

What causes the sounds that are heard in a **seashell**?

When a seashell is held to an an ear, the sounds heard are ambient, soft sounds that have been resonated and thereby amplified by the seashell's cavity. The extreme sensitivity of the human ear to sound is illustrated by the seashell resonance effect.

What is the **Doppler effect**?

The Austrian physicist, Christian Doppler (1803–1853) in 1842 explained the phenomenon of the apparent change in wavelength of radiation—such as sound or light—emitted either by a moving body (source) or by the moving receiver. The frequency of the wave-lengths increases and the wavelength becomes shorter as the moving source approaches, producing high-pitched sounds and bluish light (called blue shift). Likewise as the source recedes from the receiver the frequency of the wavelengths decreases, the sound is pitched lower and light appears reddish (called red shift). This Doppler effect is commonly demonstrated by the whistle of an approaching train or jet aircraft.

There are three differences between acoustical (sound) and optical (light) Doppler effects: The optical frequency change is not dependent on which is moving—

the source or observer—nor is it affected by the medium through which the waves are moving, but acoustical frequency is affected by such conditions. Optical frequency changes are affected if the source or observer moves at right angles to the line connecting the source and observer. Observed acoustical changes are not affected in such a situation. Applications of the Doppler phenomenon include the Doppler radar and the measurement by astronomers of the motion and direction of celestial bodies.

What is a **decibel**?

A decibel is a measure of the relative loudness or intensity of sound. A 20 decibel sound is 10 times louder than a 10 decibel sound; 30 decibels is 100 times louder, etc. One decibel is the smallest difference between sounds detectable by the human ear.

Decibel Level	Equivalent
10	Light whisper
20	Quiet conversation
30	Normal conversation
40	Light traffic
50	Typewriter, Loud conversation
60	Noisy office
70	Normal traffic, Quiet train
80	Rock music, Subway
90	Heavy traffic, Thunder
100	Jet plane at takeoff

What is the sound frequency of the **musical scale**?

EQUAL TEMPERED SCALE			
Note	Frequency	Note	Frequency
C♭	261.63	G	392.00
C#	277.18	G#	415.31
D	293.67	A	440.00
D#	311.13	A#	466.16
E	329.63	B	493.88
F	349.23	C n	523.25
F#	369.99		

Notes: ♭ indicates flat; # indicates sharp; n indicates return to natural.

The lowest frequency distinguishable as a note is about 20 hertz. The highest audible frequency is about 20,000 hertz. A hertz (symbol Hz) is a unit of frequency that measures the number of the wave cycles per second frequency of a periodic phenomenon whose periodic time is one second (cycles per second).

What is the **speed of sound**?

The speed of sound is not a constant; it varies depending on the medium in which it travels. The measurement of sound velocity in the medium of air must take into account many factors, including air temperature, pressure, and purity. At sea level and 32°F (0°C), scientists do not agree on a standard figure; estimates range from 740 to 741.5 miles (1191.6 to 1193.22 kilometers) per hour. As air temperature rises, sound velocity increases. Sound travels faster in water than in air and even faster in iron and steel. Sounds traveling a mile in air for five seconds, will travel the same distance in one second underwater and travel one-third of a second in steel.

What are the characteristics of **alpha, beta, and gamma radiation**?

Radiation is a term that describes all the ways energy is emitted by the atom as x-rays, gamma rays, neutrons, or as charged particles. Most atoms, being stable, are nonradioactive; but some are unstable and give off either particles or gamma radiation. Substances bombarded by radioactive particles can become radioactive and yield alpha particles, beta particles, and gamma rays.

Alpha particles, first identified by Antoine Henri Becquerel (1852–1908), have a positive electrical charge and consist of two protons and two neutrons. Because of their great mass, alpha particles can travel only a short distance, around two inches (five centimeters) in air, and can be stopped by a sheet of paper.

Beta particles, identified by Ernest Rutherford (1871–1937), are extremely high-speed electrons or protons that move at the speed of light. They can travel far in air and can pass through solid matter several millimeters thick.

Gamma rays, identified by Marie (1867–1934) and Pierre Curie (1859–1906), are similar to x-rays, but usually have a shorter wave length. These rays, which are bursts of protons, or very short-wave electromagnetic radiation, travel at the speed of light. They are much more penetrating than either the alpha or beta particles and can go through seven inches (18 centimeters) of lead.

MATTER

What is the **fourth state of matter**?

Plasma, a mixture of free electrons and ions or atomic nuclei, is sometimes referred to as a "fourth state of matter." Plasmas occur in thermonuclear reactions as in the sun,

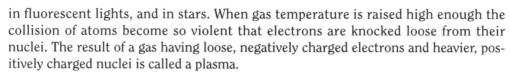

in fluorescent lights, and in stars. When gas temperature is raised high enough the collision of atoms become so violent that electrons are knocked loose from their nuclei. The result of a gas having loose, negatively charged electrons and heavier, positively charged nuclei is called a plasma.

All matter is made up of atoms. Animals and plants are organic matter; minerals and water are inorganic matter. Whether matter appears as a solid, liquid, or gas depends on how the molecules are held together in their chemical bonds. Solids have a rigid structure in the atoms of the molecules; in liquids the molecules are close together but not packed; in a gas, the molecules are widely spaced and move around, occasionally colliding but usually not interacting. These states—solid, liquid, and gas—are the first three states of matter.

Who is generally regarded as the discoverer of the electron, the proton, and the neutron?

The British physicist, Sir Joseph John Thomson (1856–1940), in 1897 researched electrical conduction in gases, which led to the important discovery that cathode rays consisted of negatively charged particles called electrons. The discovery of the electron inaugurated the electrical theory of the atom, and this with other work entitled Thomson to be regarded as the founder of modern atomic physics.

Ernest Rutherford (1871–1937) discovered the proton in 1919. He also predicted the existence of the neutron, later discovered by his colleague, James Chadwick (1891–1974). Chadwick was awarded the 1935 Nobel Prize for physics for this discovery.

How did the quark get its name?

This theoretical particle, considered to be the fundamental unit of matter, was named by Murray Gell-Mann (b. 1929) an American theoretical physicist and Nobel Prize winner. Its name was initially a playful tag that Gell-Mann invented, sounding something like "kwork." Later Gell-Mann came across the line "Three quarks for Master Marks" in James Joyce's *Finnegan's Wake*, and the tag became known as a quark. There are six kinds or

Murray Gell-Mann.

11

"flavors" (up, down, strange, charm, bottom, and top) of quarks, and each "flavor" has three varieties or "colors" (red, blue, and green). All eighteen types have different electric charges (a basic characteristic of all elementary particles). Three quarks form a proton (having one unit of positive electric charge) or a neutron (zero charge), and two quarks (a quark and an antiquark) form a meson. Like all known particles, a quark has its anti-matter opposite, known as an antiquark (having the same mass but opposite charge).

What are the **subatomic particles**?

Subatomic particles are particles that are smaller than atoms. Historically, subatomic particles were considered to be electrons, protons, and neutrons. However, the difinition of subatomic particles has now been expanded to include elementary particles, which are the particles so small that they do not appear to be made of more minute units. The physical study of such particles became possible only during the twentieth century with the development of increasingly sophisticated apparatus. Many new particles have been discovered in the last half of the twentieth century.

A number of proposals have been made to organize the particles by their spin, their mass, or their common properties. One system is now commonly known as the Standard Model. This system recognizes two basic types of fundamental particles: quarks and leptons. Other force-carrying particles are called bosons. Photons, gluons, and weakons are bosons. Leptons include electrons, muons, taus, and three kinds of neutrinos. Quarks never occur alone in nature. They always combine to form particles called hadrons. According to the Standard Model, all other subatomic particles consist of some combination of quarks and their antiparticles. A proton, for example, is thought to consist of two up quarks and their antiparticles.

What are **colligative properties**?

Colligative properties are properties of solutions that depend on the number of particles present in the solution and not on characteristics of the particles themselves. Colligative properties include depression of freezing point and elevation of boiling point. For living systems, perhaps the most important colligative property is osmotic pressure.

What substance, other than water, is **less dense as a solid** than as a liquid?

Only bismuth and water share this characteristic. Density (the mass per unit volume or mass/volume) refers to how compact or crowded a substance is. For instance, the density of water is 1 g/cm³ (gram per cubic centimeter) or 1 kg/l (kilogram per liter);

the density of a rock is 3.3 g/cm³; pure iron is 7.9 gs/cm³; and the Earth (as a whole) is 5.5 g/cm³ (average). Water as a solid (i.e., ice) floats; which is a good thing, otherwise ice would sink to the bottom of every lake or stream.

Why is **liquid water** more dense than ice?

Pure liquid water is most dense at 39.2°F (3.98°C) and decreases in density as it freezes. The water molecules in ice are held in a relatively rigid geometric pattern by their hydrogen bonds, producing an open, porous structure. Liquid water has fewer bonds; therefore, more molecules can occupy the same space, making liquid water more dense than ice.

What does **half-life** mean?

Half-life is the time it takes for the number of radioactive nuclei originally present in a sample to decrease to one half of their original number. Thus, if a sample has a half-life of one year, its radioactivity will be reduced to half its original amount at the end of a year and to one quarter at the end of two years. The half-life of a particular radionuclide is always the same, independent of temperature, chemical combination, or any other condition.

Natural radiation was discovered in 1896 by the French physicist Henri Becquerel. His discovery initiated the science of nuclear physics.

Who made the **first organic compound to be synthesized** from inorganic ingredients?

In 1828, Friedrich Wöhler (1800–1882) synthesized urea from ammonia and cyanic acid. This synthesis dealt a deathblow to the vital-force theory, which held that definite and fundamental differences existed between organic and inorganic compounds. The Swedish chemist Johan Jakob Berzelius (1779–1848) proposed that the two classes of compounds were produced from their elements by entirely different laws. Organic compounds were produced under the influence of a vital force and so were incapable of being prepared artificially. This distinction ended with Wöhler's synthesis.

Who is known as the founder of **crystallography**?

The French priest and mineralogist, René-Just Haüy (1743–1822), is called the father of crystallography. In 1781 Haüy had a fortunate accident when he dropped a piece of calcite and it broke into small fragments. He noticed that the fragments broke along straight planes that met at constant angles. He hypothesized that each crystal was

What is a chemical garden and how is one made?

Mix 4 tablespoons of bluing, 4 tablespoons of salt, and 1 tablespoon household ammonia. Pour this mixture over pieces of coal or brick in a suitable dish or bowl. Put several drops of red or green ink or mercurochrome on various parts of the coal and leave undisturbed for several days.

A crystal garden—a dishful of crystals that grow like plants and look like coral—will begin to appear. How soon the crystals will begin to appear depends on the temperatures and humidity in the room. Before long, crystals will be growing all over the briquettes, on the side of the dish, and down onto the plate. The crystals will be pure white with a snow-like texture.

built up of successive additions of what is now called a unit cell to form a simple geometric shape with constant angles. An identity or difference in crystalline form implied an identity or difference in chemical composition. This was the beginning of the science of crystallography.

By the early 1800s many physicists were experimenting with crystals; in particular, they were fascinated by their ability to bend light and separate it into its component colors. An important member of the emerging field of optical mineralogy was the British scientist David Brewster, who succeeded in classifying most known crystals according to their optical properties.

The work of French chemist Louis Pasteur during the mid 1800s became the foundation for crystal polarimetry—a method by which light is polarized, or aligned to a single plane. Pierre Curie and his brother Jacques discovered another phenomenon displayed by certain crystals called piezoelectricity. It is the creation of an electrical potential by squeezing certain crystals.

Perhaps the most important application of crystals is in the science of x-ray crystallography. Experiments in this field were first conducted by the German physicist Max von Laue. This work was perfected by William Henry Bragg (1862–1942) and William Lawrence Bragg (1890–1971) who were awarded the Nobel Prize in physics for their work. The synthesis of penicillin and insulin were made possible by the use of x-ray crystallography.

CHEMICAL ELEMENTS, ETC.

See also: Metals and Other Materials

Who are some of the **founders of modern chemistry?**

Several contenders share this honor:

Swedish chemist Jöns Jakob Berzelius (1779–1848) devised chemical symbols, determined atomic weights, contributed to the atomic theory, and discovered several new elements. Between 1810 and 1816, he described the preparation, purification, and analysis of 2,000 chemical compounds. Then he determined atomic weights for 40 elements. He simplified chemical symbols, introducing a notation (still used today)—letters with numbers—that replaced the pictorial symbols his predecessors used. He discovered cerium (in 1803, with Wilhelm Hisinger), selenium (1818), silicon (1824), and thorium (1829).

Robert Boyle (1627–1691), a British natural philosopher, is considered one of the founders of modern chemistry. Best known for his discovery of Boyle's Law (volume of a gas is inversely proportional to its pressure at constant temperature), he was a pioneer in the use of experiments and the scientific method. A founder of the Royal Society, he worked to remove the mystique of alchemy from chemistry to make it a pure science.

The French chemist Antoine-Laurent Lavoisier (1743–1794) is regarded as another founder of modern chemistry. His wide-ranging contributions include the discrediting of the phlogiston theory of combustion, which had been for so long a stumbling block to a true understanding of chemistry. He established modern terminology for chemical substances and did the first experiments in quantitative organic analysis. He is sometimes credited with having discovered or established the law of conservation of mass in chemical reactions.

John Dalton (1766–1844), an English chemist, proposed an atomic theory of matter that became a basic theory of modern chemistry. His theory, first proposed in 1803, states that each chemical element is composed of its own kind of atoms, all with the same relative weight.

Who developed the **periodic table?**

Dmitri Ivanovich Mendeleyev (1834–1907) was a Russian chemist whose name will always be linked with his outstanding achievement, the development of the periodic table. He was the first chemist really to understand that all elements are related members of a single ordered system. He changed what had been a highly fragmented and speculative branch of chemistry into a true, logical science. His nomination for the 1906 Nobel Prize for chemistry failed by one vote, but his name became recorded in perpetuity 50 years later when element 101 was called mendelevium.

According to Mendeleyev, the properties of the elements, as well as those of their compounds, are periodic functions of their atomic weights (in the 1920s, it was discovered that atomic number was the key rather than weight). Mendeleyev compiled the first true periodic table listing all the 63 (then-known) elements. In order to make the table work, Mendeleyev had to leave gaps, and he predicted that further elements would eventually be discovered to fill them. Three were discovered in Mendeleyev's lifetime: gallium, scandium, and germanium.

Dimitri Mendeleyev.

There are 94 naturally occurring elements; of the 15 remaining elements (elements 95 to 109), 10 are undisputed. By 1984, over 6.8 million chemical compounds had been produced from these elements; 65 thousand of them in common use.

What are the **alkali metals**?

These are the elements at the left of the periodic table: lithium (Li, element 3), potassium (K, element 19), rubidium (Rb, element 37), cesium (Cs, element 55), francium (Fr, element 87), and sodium (Na, element 11). The alkali metals are sometimes called the sodium family of elements, or Group I elements. Because of their great chemical reactivity (easily form positive ions), none exist in nature in the elemental state.

What are the **alkaline Earth metals**?

These are beryllium (Be, element 4), magnesium (Mg, element 12), calcium (Ca, element 20), strontium (Sr, element 38), barium (Ba, element 56), and radium (Ra, element 88). The alkaline Earth metals are also called Group II elements. Like the alkali metals, they are never found as free elements in nature and are moderately reactive metals. Harder and less volatile than the alkali metals, these elements all burn in air.

What are the **transition elements**?

The transition elements are the 10 subgroups of elements between Group II and Group XIII, starting with period 4. They include gold (Au, element 79), silver (Ag, element 47), platinum (Pt, element 78), iron (Fe, element 26), copper (Cu, element 29), and other metals. All transition elements are metals. Compared to alkali and alkaline Earth met-

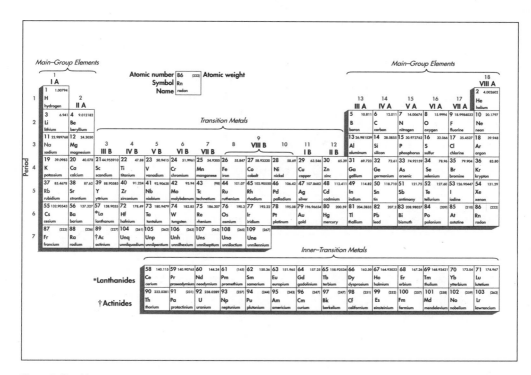

The periodic table.

als, they are usually harder and more brittle and have higher melting points. Transition metals are also good conductors of heat and electricity. They have variable valences, and compounds of transition elements are often colored. Transition elements are so named because they comprise a gradual shift from the strongly electropositive elements of Groups I and II to the electronegative elements of Groups VI and VII.

What are the **transuranic chemical elements** and the currently proposed names for elements 102–109?

Transuranium elements are those elements in the periodic system with atomic numbers greater than 92. The names for elements 102–109 have been under review by the International Union of Pure & Applied Chemistry (IUPAC).

Elements 93–103

Element Number	Name	Symbol
93	Neptunium	Np
94	Plutonium	Pu

Element Number	Name	Symbol
95	Americum	Am
96	Curium	Cm
97	Berkelium	Bk
98	Californium	Cf
99	Einsteinium	Es
100	Fermium	Fm
101	Mendelevium	Md

Elements 102–109

Element Number	Proposed Names (by discovery group)	IUPAC name	Symbol
102	Nobelium (Swedish) Joliotium (Russian)	Nobelium	No
103	Lawrencium (American)	Lawrencium	Lr
104	Rutherfordium (American) Kurchatovium (Russian)	Dubnium	Db
105	Hahnium (American) Nielsbohrium (Russian)	Joliotium	Jl
106	Seaborgium (American)	Rutherfordium	Rf
107	Nielsborium (German)	Bohrium	Bh
108	Hassium (German)	Hahnium	Hn
109	Meitnerium (German)	Meitnerium	Mt

Which elements are the "noble metals"?

The noble metals are gold (Au, element 79), silver (Ag, element 47), mercury (Hg, element 80), and the platinum group, which includes platinum (Pt, element 78), palladium (Pd, element 46), iridium (Ir, element 77), rhodium (Rh, element 45), ruthenium (Ru, element 44), and osmium (Os, element 76). The term refers to those metals highly resistant to chemical reaction or oxidation (resistant to corrosion) and is contrasted to "base" metals, which are not so resistant. The term has its origins in ancient alchemy whose goals of transformation and perfection were pursued through the different properties of metals and chemicals. The term is not synonymous with "precious metals," although a metal, like platinum, may be both.

The platinum group metals have a variety of uses. In the United States more than 95% of all platinum group metals are used for industrial purposes. While platinum is a coveted material for jewelry making, it is also used in the catalytic converters of automobiles to control exhaust emissions, as are rhodium and palladium. Rhodium can also be alloyed with platinum and palladium for use in furnace windings, thermocouple elements and in aircraft spark-plug electrodes. Osmium is used in the manufacture of pharmaceuticals and in alloys for instrument pivots and long-life phonograph needles.

What is a philosopher's stone?

A philosopher's stone was the name of a substance believed by medieval alchemists to have the power to change baser metals into gold or silver. It had, according to some, the power of prolonging life and of curing all injuries and diseases. The pursuit of it by alchemists led to the discovery of several chemical substances; however, the magical philosopher's stone has since proved fictitious.

What are some chemical elements whose **symbols** are not derived from their English names?

Modern Name	Symbol	Older Name
antimony	Sb	stibium
copper	Cu	cuprum
gold	Au	aurum
iron	Fe	ferrum
lead	Pb	plumbum
mercury	Hg	hydrargyrum
potassium	K	kalium
silver	Ag	argentum
sodium	Na	natrium
tin	Sn	stannum
tungsten	W	wolfram

Which elements are **liquid at room temperature?**

Mercury ("liquid silver," Hg, element 80) and bromine (Br, element 35) are liquid at room temperature 68° to 70°F (20° to 25°C). Gallium (Ga, element 31) with a melting point of 85.6°F (29.8°C) and cesium (Cs, element 55) with a melting point of 83°F (28.4°C), are liquids at slightly above room temperature.

What is **Harkin's rule?**

Atoms having even atomic numbers are more abundant in the universe than are atoms having odd atomic numbers. Chemical properties of an element are determined by its atomic number, which is the number of protons in the atom's nucleus.

Which chemical element is the **most abundant in the universe**?

Hydrogen (H, element 1) makes up about 75% of the mass of the universe. It is estimated that more than 90% of all atoms in the universe are hydrogen atoms. Most of the rest are helium (He, element 2) atoms.

Which chemical elements are the **most abundant on Earth**?

Oxygen (O, element 8) is the most abundant element in the Earth's crust, waters, and atmosphere. It composes 49.5% of the total mass of these compounds. Silicon (Si, element 14) is the second most abundant element. Silicon dioxide and silicates make up about 87% of the materials in the Earth's crust.

Why are the **rare gases** and **rare Earth elements** called "rare"?

Rare gases refers to the elements helium, neon, argon, krypton, and xenon. They are rare in that they are gases of very low density ("rarified") at ordinary temperatures and are found only scattered in minute quantities in the atmosphere and in some substances. In addition, rare gases have zero valence and normally will not combine with other elements to make compounds.

Rare Earth elements are elements numbered 58 through 71 in the periodic table plus yttrium (Y, element 39) and thorium (Th, element 90). They are called "rare Earths" because they are difficult to extract from monazite ore, where they occur. The term has nothing to do with scarcity or rarity in nature.

Which elements have the **most isotopes**?

The elements with the most isotopes, with 36 each, are xenon (Xe) with nine stable isotopes (identified from 1920 to 1922) and 27 radioactive isotopes (identified from 1939 to 1981), and cesium (Cs) with one stable isotope (identified in 1921) and 35 radioactive isotopes (identified from 1935 to 1983).

The element with the least number of isotopes is hydrogen (H), with three isotopes, including two stable ones—protium (identified in 1920) and deuterium (identified in 1931)—and one radioactive isotope—tritium (first identified in 1934, but later considered a radioactive isotope in 1939).

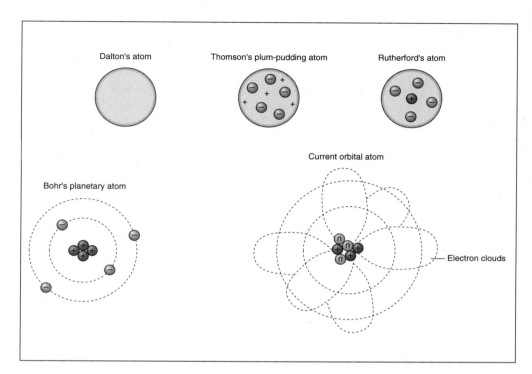

Hydrogen isotopes.

Which element has the **highest density**?

Either osmium or iridium is the element with the highest density; however, scientists have yet to gather enough conclusive data to choose between the two. When traditional methods of measurement are employed, osmium generally appears to be the densest element. Yet, when calculations are made based upon the space lattice, which may be a more reliable method given the nature of these elements, the density of iridium is 22.65 compared to 22.61 for osmium.

What is the **density of air**?

The density of dry air is 1.29 grams per liter at 32°F (0°C) at average sea level and a barometric pressure of 29.92 inches of mercury (760 millimeters).

The weight of one cubic foot of dry air at one atmosphere of barometric pressure is:

Temperature (Fahrenheit)	Weight per cubic foot (pounds)
50°	0.07788
60°	0.07640
70°	0.07495

What is **heavy water**?

Heavy water, also called deuterium oxide (D_2O), is composed of oxygen and two hydrogen atoms in the form of deuterium, which has about twice the mass of normal hydrogen. As a result, heavy water has a molecular weight of about 20, while ordinary water has a molecular weight of about 18. Approximately one part heavy water can be found in 6,500 parts of ordinary water, and it may be extracted by fractional distillation. It is used in thermonuclear weapons and nuclear reactors and as an isotopic tracer in studies of chemical and biochemical processes.

What is a **Lewis acid**?

Named after the American chemist Gilbert Newton Lewis (1875–1946), the Lewis theory defines an *acid* as a species that can accept an electron pair from another atom, and a *base* as a species that can donate an electron pair to complete the valence shell of another atom. Hydrogen ion (proton) is the simplest substance that will do this, but Lewis acids include many compounds—such as boron trifluoride (BF_3) and aluminum chloride ($AlCl_3$)—that can react with ammonia, for example, to form an addition compound or Lewis salt.

What are the **gas laws**?

The gas laws are physical laws concerning the behavior of gases. They include *Boyle's law,* which states that the volume of a given mass of gas at a constant temperature is inversely proportional to its pressure; and *Charles's law,* which states that the volume of a given mass of gas at constant pressure is directly proportional to its absolute temperature. These two laws can be combined to give the *General* or *Universal gas law,* which may be expressed as:

$$\frac{(\text{pressure} \times \text{volume})}{\text{temperature}} = \text{constant}$$

Avogardro's law states that equal volumes of all gases contain the same number of particles if they all have the same pressure and temperature.

The laws are not obeyed exactly by any real gas, but many common gases obey them under certain conditions, particularly at high temperatures and low pressures.

Which chemical is **used in greater quantities** than any other?

Sodium chloride (NaCl), or salt, has over 14,000 uses, and is probably used in greater quantities and for more applications than any other chemical.

Which chemicals are used today as **embalming fluids**?

During the 19th century embalming became a common practice in the United States, and generally salts of heavy metals such as arsenic, antimony, lead, mercury, and copper were used to preserve the corpse and inhibit bacterial growth. By the early 1900s, however, laws were passed prohibiting the use of metal salts in embalming. Formaldehyde soon became the compound of choice and continues to be the most common preservative in embalming fluids. Its continued popularity is due to low cost, availability in usable form, and simplicity of use. It also provides good cell preservation under a variety of pH conditions. Generally, a mortician, after draining the corpse of bodily fluids, injects it with a solution of formaldehyde in water. Various buffers are also present in the solution to counteract the formation of "formaldehyde pigments" on the body. Concerns over the possible carcinogenic effects of formaldehyde, as well as its tendancy to turn a corpse's skin an ashen grey, have instigated numerous attempts at finding a replacement. Glutaraldehyde was first used in 1955, but in spite of some distinct advantages, formaldehyde is still the embalming fluid of choice.

MEASUREMENT, METHODOLOGY, ETC.

What were some of the leading contributions of **Albert Einstein**?

Albert Einstein (1879–1955) was the principal founder of modern theoretical physics; his theory of relativity (speed of light is a constant and not relative to the observer or source of light), and the relationship of mass and energy ($e=mc^2$), fundamentally changed human understanding of the physical world.

During a single year in 1905, he produced three landmark papers. These papers dealt with the nature of particle movement known as Brownian motion, the quantum nature of electromagnetic radiation as demonstrated by the photoelectric effect, and the special theory of relativity. Although Einstein is probably best known for the last of these works, it was for his quantum explanation of the photoelectric effect that he was awarded the 1921 Nobel Prize in physics. His stature as a scientist, together with his strong humanitarian stance on major

Albert Einstein.

political and social issues, made him one of the outstanding men of the twentieth century.

Who is generally regarded as the founder of quantum mechanics?

The German mathematical physicist, Werner Karl Heisenberg (1901–1976), is regarded as the father of quantum mechanics (theory of small-scale physical phenomena). His theory of uncertainty in 1927 overturned traditional classical mechanics and electromagnetic theory regarding energy and motions when applied to subatomic particles such as electrons and parts of atomic nuclei. The theory states that it is impossible to specify precisely both the position and the simultaneous momentum (mass × volume) of a particle, but they could only be predicted. This meant that a result of an action can only be expressed in terms of probability that a certain effect will occur, not certainty.

Werner Karl Heisenberg.

Who invented the thermometer?

The Greeks of Alexandria knew that air expanded as it was heated, and it is known that Hero of Alexandria (first century C.E.) and Philo of Byzantium made simple thermometers or "thermoscopes," but they were not real thermometers. In 1592, Galileo (1564–1642) made a kind of thermometer that also functioned as a barometer, but in 1612, his friend Santorio Santorio (1561–1636) first adapted the air thermometer (a device in which a colored liquid was driven down by the expansion of air) to measure the body's temperature change during illness and recovery. Still, it was not until 1713 that Daniel Fahrenheit (1686–1736) began developing a thermometer having a fixed scale. He worked out his scale from two "fixed" points: the melting point of ice and the heat of the healthy human body. He realized that the melting point of ice was a constant temperature, whereas the freezing point of water varied. Fahrenheit put his thermometer into a mixture of ice, water, and salt (which he marked off as 0°) and using this as a starting point, marked off melting ice at 32° and blood heat at 96°. In 1835, it was discovered that normal blood measured 98.6°F. Sometimes, Fahrenheit used spirit of wine as the liquid in the thermometer tube, but more often he used specially purified mercury. Later, the boiling point of water (212°F) became the upper fixed point.

What is the **Kelvin** temperature scale?

Temperature is the level of heat in a gas, liquid, or solid. The freezing and boiling points of water are used as standard reference levels in both the metric (centigrade or Celsius) and the English system (Fahrenheit). In the metric system, the difference between freezing and boiling is divided into 100 equal intervals called degree Celsius or degree centigrade (°C). In the English system, the intervals are divided into 180 units, with one unit called degree Fahrenheit (°F). But temperature can be measured from absolute zero (no heat, no motion); this principle defines thermodynamic temperature and establishes a method to measure it upward. This scale of temperature is called the Kelvin temperature scale, after its inventor, William Thomson, Lord Kelvin (1824–1907), who devised it in 1848. The Kelvin (symbol K) has the same magnitude as the degree Celsius (the difference between freezing and boiling water is 100 degrees), but the two temperatures differ by 273.15 degrees (absolute zero, which is -273.15°C on the Celsius scale). Below is a comparison of the three temperatures:

Characteristic	K°	C°	F°
Absolute zero	0	-273.15	-459.67
Freezing point of water	273.15	0	32
Normal human body temperature	310.15	37	98.6
Boiling point of water	373.15	100	212

To convert Celsius to Kelvin: Add 273.15 to the temperature($K = C + 273.15$). To convert Fahrenheit to Celsius: Subtract 32 from the temperature and multiply the difference by 5; then divide the product by 9 ($C = 5/9[F - 32]$). To convert Celsius to Fahrenheit: Multiply the temperature by 1.8, then add 32 ($F = 9/5C + 32$ or $F = 1.8C + 32$).

What was unusual about the original **Celsius** temperature scale?

In 1742, the Swedish astronomer Anders Celsius (1701–1744) set the freezing point of water at 100°C and the boiling point of water at 0°C. It was Carolus Linnaeus (1707–1778), who reversed the scale, but a later textbook attributed the modified scale to Celsius and the name has remained.

How are **Celsius** temperatures **converted into Fahrenheit** temperatures?

The formulas for converting Celsius or Centigrade temperatures into Fahrenheit (and the reverse) are as follows:

$$F = (C \times 9/5) + 32$$
$$C = (F - 32) \times 5/9$$

Some useful comparisons of the two scales:

Temperature	Fahrenheit	Celsius or Centigrade
Absolute zero	-459.67	-273.15
Point of equality	-40.0	-40.0
Zero fahrenheit	0.0	-17.8
Freezing point of water	32.0	0.0
Normal human blood temperature	98.4	36.9
100 degrees F	100.0	37.8
Boiling point of water (at standard pressure)	212.0	100.0

What is **STP**?

The abbreviation STP is often used for *standard temperature* and *pressure*. As a matter of convenience, scientists have chosen a specific temperature and pressure as standards for comparing gas volumes. The standard temperature is 0°C (273°K) and the standard pressure is 760 torr (one atmosphere).

How did the electrical term **ampere** originate?

It was named for André Marie Ampère (1775–1836), the physicist who formulated the basic laws of the science of electrodynamics. The *ampere* (symbol A), often abbreviated as "amp," is the unit of electric current, defined at the constant current, that, maintained in two straight parallel infinite conductors placed one meter apart in a vacuum, would produce a force between the conductors of 2×10^{-7} newton per meter. For example, the amount of current flowing through a 100-watt light bulb is 1 amp; through a toaster, 10 amps; a TV set, 3 amps; a car battery, 50 amps (while cranking). A newton (symbol N) is defined as a unit of force needed to accelerate one kilogram by one meter second^{-2}, or $1N = 1Kg^{MS-2}$.

How did the electrical unit **volt** originate?

The unit of voltage is the volt, named after Alessandro Volta (1745–1827), the Italian scientist who built the first modern battery. (A battery, operating with a lead rod and vinegar, was also manufactured in Egypt several thousand years ago.) Voltage measures the force or "oomph" with which electrical charges are pushed through a material. Some common voltages are 1.5 volts for a flashlight battery; 12 volts for a car battery; 115 volts for ordinary household receptacles and 230 volts for a heavy-duty household receptacle.

How did the electrical unit **watt** originate?

Named for the Scottish engineer and inventor James Watt (1736–1819), the watt is used to measure electric power. An electric device uses one watt when one volt of electric current drives one ampere of current through it.

What is a **mole** in chemistry?

A mole (symbol Mol), a fundamental measuring unit for the amount of a substance, refers to either a gram atomic weight or a gram molecular weight of a substance. It is the quantity of a substance that contains 6.02×10^{23} atoms, molecules, or formula units of that substance. This number is called Avogadro's number or constant after Amedeo Avogadro (1776–1856) who is considered to be one of the founders of physical science.

What is **Mole Day**?

Mole Day was organized by the National Mole Day Foundation to promote an awareness and enthusiasm for chemistry. It is celebrated each year on October 23rd.

How does **gram atomic weight** differ from **gram formula weight**?

Gram atomic weight is the amount of an *element* (substance made up of atoms having the same atomic number) equal to its atomic weight (the number of protons) in grams. Gram formula weight is an amount of a *compound* (a combination of elements) equal to its formula weight in grams.

SPACE

UNIVERSE

What was the **Big Bang**?

The Big Bang theory is the explanation most commonly accepted by astronomers for the origin of the universe. It proposes that the universe began as the result of an explosion—the Big Bang—15 to 20 billion years ago. Two observations form the basis of this cosmology. First, as Edwin Hubble (1889–1953) demonstrated, the universe is expanding uniformly, with objects at greater distances receding at greater velocities. Secondly, the Earth is bathed in a glow of radiation that has the characteristics expected from a remnant of a hot primeval fireball. This radiation was discovered by Arno A. Penzias (b. 1933) and Robert W. Wilson (b. 1936) of Bell Telephone Laboratories. In time, the matter created by the Big Bang came together in huge clumps to form the galaxies. Smaller clumps within the galaxies formed stars. Parts of at least one clump became a group of planets—our solar system.

How **old** is the **universe**?

Recent data collected by the Hubble Space Telescope suggests that the universe may only be eight billion years old. This contradicts the previous belief the universe was somewhere between 15 billion and 20 billion years old. The earlier figure was derived from the concept that the universe has been expanding at the same rate since its birth at the Big Bang. The rate of expansion is a ratio known as Hubble's constant. It is calculated by dividing the speed at which the galaxy is moving away from the Earth by its distance from the Earth. By inverting Hubble's Constant, that is, dividing the distance of a galaxy by its recessional speed, the age of the universe can be calculated. The estimates of both the velocity and distance of galaxies from the Earth are subject to uncertainties and not all scientists accept that the universe has always expanded at the same rate. Therefore, many still hold that the age of the universe is open to question.

Who is **Stephen Hawking?**

Hawking (b. 1943), a British physicist and mathematician, is considered to be the greatest theoretical physicist of the late 20th century. In spite of being severely handicapped by amyotrophic lateral sclerosis (ALS), he has made major contributions to scientific knowledge about black holes and the origin and evolution of the universe though his research into the nature of space-time and its anomalies. For instance, Hawking proposed that a black hole could emit thermal radiation and predicted that a black hole would disappear after all its mass has been converted into radiation (called "Hawking's radiation"). A current objective of Hawking is to synthesize quantum mechanics and relativity theory into a theory of quantum gravity. He is also the author of several books, including the popular best-selling work *A Brief History of Time*.

What are **quasars?**

The name quasar is short for *quasi-stellar radio source*. Quasars appear to be stars, but they have large red shifts in their spectra indicating that they are receding from the Earth at great speeds, some at up to 90% of the speed of light. Their exact nature is still unknown, but many believe quasars to be the cores of distant galaxies, the most distant objects yet seen. Quasars were first identified in 1963 by astronomers at the Palomar Observatory in California.

What is a **syzygy?**

A syzygy is a configuration that occurs when three celestial bodies lie in a straight line, such as the sun, Earth, and moon during a solar or lunar eclipse. The particular syzygy when a planet is on the opposite side of the Earth from the sun is called an opposition.

Which **galaxy** is closest to us?

The Andromeda Galaxy is the galaxy closest to the Milky Way galaxy, where Earth is located. It is estimated to be 2.2 million light years away from Earth. Bigger than the Milky Way, Andromeda is a spiral-shaped galaxy that is also the brightest in Earth's sky.

STARS

What is a **binary star**?

A binary star is a pair of stars revolving around a common center of gravity. About half of all stars are members of either binary star systems or multiple star systems, which contain more than two stars.

The bright star Sirius, about 8.6 light years away, is composed of two stars, one about 2.3 times the mass of the sun, the other a white dwarf star about 980 times the mass of Jupiter. Alpha Centauri, the nearest star to Earth after the sun, is actually three stars: Alpha Centauri A and Alpha Centauri B, two sunlike stars, orbit each other, and Alpha Centauri C, a low mass red star, orbits around them.

What is a black hole?

When a star with a mass greater than about four times that of the sun collapses even the neutrons cannot stop the force of gravity. There is nothing to stop the contraction and the star collapses forever. The material is so dense that nothing—not even light—can escape. The American physicist John Wheeler, in 1967, gave this phenomenon the name "black hole." Since no light escapes from a black hole, it cannot be observed directly. However, if a black hole existed near another star, it would draw matter from the other star into itself and, in effect, produce x-rays. In the constellation of Cygnus, there is a strong x-ray source, named Cygnus X-1. It is near a star, and the two revolve around each other. The unseen x-ray source has the gravitational pull of at least 10 suns and is believed to be a black hole. Another type of black hole, a primordial black hole, may also exist dating from the time of the Big Bang when regions of gas and dust were highly compressed.

There are four other possible black holes: a Schwarzschild black hole has no charge and no angular momentum; a Reissner-Nordstrom black hole has charge but no angular momentum; a Kerr black hole has angular momentum but no charge; and a Kerr-Newman black hole has charge and angular momentum.

What is a **pulsar**?

A pulsar is a rotating neutron star that gives off sharp regular pulses of radio waves at rates ranging from 0.001 to four seconds. Stars burn by fusing hydrogen into helium. When they use up their hydrogen, their interiors begin to contract. During this contraction, energy is released and the outer layers of the star are pushed out. These layers are large and cool; the star is now a red giant. A star with more than twice the mass of the sun will continue to expand, becoming a supergiant. At that point, it may blow up in an explosion called a supernova. After a supernova, the remaining material of the star's core may be so compressed that the electrons and protons become neutrons. A star 1.4 to four times the mass of the sun can be compressed into a neutron star only about 12 miles (20 kilometers) across. Neutron stars rotate very fast. The neutron star at the center of the Crab Nebula spins 30 times per second.

A pulsar is formed by the collapse of a star with 1.4 to four times the mass of the sun. Some of these neutron stars emit radio signals from their magnetic poles in a direction that reaches Earth. These signals were first detected by Jocelyn Bell (b. 1943) of Cambridge University in 1967. Because of their regularity some people speculated that they were extraterrestrial beacons constructed by alien civilizations. This theory was eventually ruled out and the rotating neutron star came to be accepted as the explanation for these pulsating radio sources, or pulsars.

What does the **color of a star** indicate?

The color of a star gives an indication of its temperature and age. Stars are classified by their spectral type. From oldest to youngest and hottest to coolest, the types of stars are:

| Type | Color | Temperature | |
		Farenheit	Celsius
O	Blue	45,000–75,000	25,000–40,000
B	Blue	20,800–45,000	11,000–25,000
A	Blue-White	13,500–20,000	7,500–11,000
F	White	10,800–13,500	6,000–7,500
G	Yellow	9,000–10,800	5,000–6,000
K	Orange	6,300–9,000	3,500–5,000
M	Red	5,400–6,300	3,000–3,500

Each type is further subdivided on a scale of 0–9. The sun is a type G2 star.

Which stars are the **brightest**?

The brightness of a star is called its magnitude. Apparent magnitude is how bright a star appears to the naked eye. The lower the magnitude, the brighter the star. On a

clear night, stars of about magnitude +6 can be seen with the naked eye. Large telescopes can detect objects as faint as +27. Very bright objects have negative magnitudes; the sun is -26.8.

Star	Constellation	Apparent Magnitude
Sirius	Canis Major	-1.47
Canopus	Carina	-0.72
Arcturus	Boötes	-0.06
Rigil Kentaurus	Centaurus	+0.01
Vega	Lyra	+0.04
Capella	Auriga	+0.05
Rigel	Orion	+0.14
Procyon	Canis Minor	+0.37
Betelgeuse	Orion	+0.41
Achernar	Eridanus	+0.51

What is the **Milky Way**?

The Milky Way is a hazy band of light that can be seen encircling the night sky. This light comes from the stars that make up the Milky Way galaxy, the galaxy to which the sun and the Earth belong. Galaxies are huge systems of stars separated from one another by largely empty space. Astronomers estimate that the Milky Way galaxy contains at least 100 billion stars and is about 100,000 light years in diameter. The galaxy is shaped like a phonograph record with a central bulge, or nucleus, and spiral arms curving out from the center.

What is the **Big Dipper**?

The Big Dipper is a group of seven stars that are part of the constellation Ursa Major. They appear to form a sort of spoon with a long handle. The group is known as the Plough in Great Britain. The Big Dipper is almost always visible in the northern hemisphere. It serves as a convenient reference point when locating other stars; for example, an imaginary line drawn from the two end stars of the dipper leads to Polaris, the North Star.

Where is the **North Star**?

If an imaginary line is drawn from the North Pole into space, it will reach a star called Polaris, or the North Star, less than one degree away from the line. As the Earth rotates on its axis, Polaris acts as a pivot-point around which all the stars visible in the northern hemisphere appear to move, while Polaris itself remains motionless.

What is the **summer triangle**?

The summer triangle is the triangle formed by the stars Deneb, Vega, and Altair as seen in the summer Milky Way.

How many **constellations** are there and how were they named?

Constellations are groups of stars that seem to form some particular shape, that of a person, animal, or object. They only appear to form this shape and be close to each other from Earth; in actuality the stars in a constellation are often very distant from each other. There are 88 recognized constellations whose boundaries were defined in the 1920s by the International Astronomical Union.

Various cultures in all parts of the world have had their own constellations. However, because modern science is predominantly a product of Western culture, many of the constellations represent characters from Greek and Roman mythology. When Europeans began to explore the southern hemisphere in the 16th and 17th centuries, they derived some of the new star patterns from the technological wonders of their time, such as the microscope.

Names of constellations are usually given in Latin. Individual stars in a constellation are usually designated with Greek letters in the order of brightness; the brightest star is alpha, the second brightest is beta, and so on. The genitive, or possessive, form of the constellation name is used, thus Alpha Orionis is the brightest star of the constellation Orion.

Constellation	Genitive	Abbreviation	Meaning
Andromeda	Andromedae	And	Chained Maiden
Antlia	Antliae	Ant	Air Pump
Apus	Apodis	Aps	Bird of Paradise
Aquarius	Aquarii	Aqr	Water Bearer
Aquila	Aquilae	Aql	Eagle
Ara	Arae	Ara	Altar
Aries	Arietis	Ari	Ram
Auriga	Aurigae	Aur	Charioteer
Boötes	Boötis	Boo	Herdsman
Caelum	Caeli	Cae	Chisel
Camelopardalis	Camelopardalis	Cam	Giraffe
Cancer	Cancri	Cnc	Crab
Canes Venatici	Canum Venaticorum	CVn	Hunting Dogs
Canis Major	Canis Majoris	CMa	Big Dog
Canis Minor	Canis Minoris	CMi	Little Dog

Capricornus	Capricorni	Cap	Goat
Carina	Carinae	Car	Ship's Keel
Cassiopeia	Cassiopeiae	Cas	Queen of Ethiopia
Centaurus	Centauri	Cen	Centaur
Cepheus	Cephei	Cep	King of Ethiopia
Cetus	Ceti	Cet	Whale
Chamaeleon	Chamaeleonis	Cha	Chameleon
Circinus	Circini	Cir	Compass
Columba	Columbae	Col	Dove
Coma Berenices	Comae Berenices	Com	Berenice's Hair
Corona Australis	Coronae Australis	CrA	Southern Crown
Corona Borealis	Coronae Borealis	CrB	Northern Crown
Corvus	Corvi	Crv	Crow
Crater	Crateris	Crt	Cup
Crux	Crucis	Cru	Southern Cross
Cygnus	Cygni	Cyg	Swan
Delphinus	Delphini	Del	Dolphin
Dorado	Doradus	Dor	Goldfish
Draco	Draconis	Dra	Dragon
Equuleus	Equulei	Equ	Little Horse
Eridanus	Eridani	Eri	River Eridanus
Fornax	Fornacis	For	Furnace
Gemini	Geminorum	Gem	Twins
Grus	Gruis	Gru	Crane
Hercules	Herculis	Her	Hercules
Horologium	Horologii	Hor	Clock
Hydra	Hydrae	Hya	Hydra, Greek monster
Hydrus	Hydri	Hyi	Sea Serpent
Indus	Indi	Ind	Indian
Lacerta	Lacertae	Lac	Lizard
Leo	Leonis	Leo	Lion
Leo Minor	Leonis Minoris	LMi	Little Lion
Lepus	Leporis	Lep	Hare
Libra	Librae	Lib	Scales
Lupus	Lupi	Lup	Wolf
Lynx	Lyncis	Lyn	Lynx
Lyra	Lyrae	Lyr	Lyre or Harp
Mensa	Mensae	Men	Table Mountain
Microscopium	Microscopii	Mic	Microscope
Monoceros	Monocerotis	Mon	Unicorn
Musca	Muscae	Mus	Fly
Norma	Normae	Nor	Carpenter's Square
Octans	Octanis	Oct	Octant

Constellation	Genitive	Abbreviation	Meaning
Ophiuchus	Ophiuchi	Oph	Serpent Bearer
Orion	Orionis	Ori	Orion, the Hunter
Pavo	Pavonis	Pav	Peacock
Pegasus	Pegasi	Peg	Winged Horse
Perseus	Persei	Per	Perseus, a Greek hero
Phoenix	Phoenicis	Phe	Phoenix
Pictor	Pictoris	Pic	Painter
Pisces	Piscium	Psc	Fish
Piscis Austrinus	Piscis Austrini	PsA	Southern Fish
Puppis	Puppis	Pup	Ship's Stern
Pyxis	Pyxidis	Pyx	Ship's Compass
Reticulum	Reticuli	Ret	Net
Sagitta	Sagittae	Sge	Arrow
Sagittarius	Sagittarii	Sgr	Archer
Scorpius	Scorpii	Sco	Scorpion
Sculptor	Sculptoris	Scl	Sculptor
Scutum	Scuti	Sct	Shield
Serpens	Serpentis	Ser	Serpent
Sextans	Sextantis	Sex	Sextant
Taurus	Tauri	Tau	Bull
Telescopium	Telescopii	Tel	Telescope
Triangulum	Trianguli	Tri	Triangle
Triangulum	Triangli Australis	TrA	Southern Australe Triangle
Tucana	Tucanae	Tuc	Toucan
Ursa Major	Ursae Majoris	UMa	Big Bear
Ursa Minor	Ursae Minoris	UMi	Little Bear
Vela	Velorum	Vel	Ship's Sail
Virgo	Virginis	Vir	Virgin
Volans	Volantis	Vol	Flying Fish
Vulpecula	Vulpeculae	Vul	Little Fox

What is the **largest constellation?**

Hydra is the largest constellation, extending from Gemini to the south of Virgo. It has a recognizable long line of stars. The name "hydra" is derived from the watersnake monster killed by Hercules in ancient mythology.

Which star is the **closest to Earth?**

The sun, at a distance of 92,955,900 miles (149,598,000 kilometers), is the closest star to the Earth. After the sun, the closest stars are the members of the triple star system known as Alpha Centauri (Alpha Centauri A, Alpha Centauri B, and Alpha Centauri C, sometimes called Proxima Centauri). They are 4.3 light years away.

What is the **sun made of**?

The sun is an incandescent ball of gases. Its mass is 1.8×10^{27} tons or 1.8 octillion tons (a mass 330,000 times as great as the Earth).

Element	% of mass
Hydrogen	73.46
Helium	24.85
Oxygen	0.77
Carbon	0.29
Iron	0.16
Neon	0.12
Nitrogen	0.09
Silicon	0.07
Magnesium	0.05
Sulfur	0.04
Other	0.10

How **hot** is the sun?

The center of the sun is about 27,000,000°F (15,000,000°C). The surface, or photosphere, of the sun is about 10,000°F (5,500°C). Magnetic anomolies in the photosphere cause cooler regions that appear to be darker than the surrounding surface. These sunspots are about 6,700°F (4,000°C). The sun's layer of lower atmosphere, the chromosphere, is only a few thousand miles thick. At the base, the chromosphere is about 7,800°F (4,300°C), but its temperature rises with altitude to the corona, the sun's outer layer of atmosphere, which has a temperature of about 1,800,000°F (1,000,000°C).

When will the **sun die**?

The sun is approximately 4.5 billion years old. About five billion years from now, the sun will have burned all of its hydrogen fuel into helium. As this process occurs, the sun will change from the yellow dwarf as we know it to a red giant. Its diameter will extend well beyond the orbit of Venus, and even possibly beyond the orbit of Earth. In either case, the Earth will be burned to a cinder.

What is the **ecliptic**?

Ecliptic refers to the apparent yearly path of the sun through the sky with respect to **37** the stars. In the spring, the ecliptic in the northern hemisphere is angled high in the evening sky. In fall, the ecliptic lies much closer to the horizon.

Why does the **color of the sun** vary?

Sunlight contains all the colors of the rainbow, which blend to form white light, making sunlight appear white. At times, some of the color wavelengths, especially blue, become scattered in the Earth's atmosphere and the sunlight appears colored. When the sun is high in the sky, some of the blue rays are scattered in the Earth's atmosphere. At such times, the sky looks blue and the sun appears to be yellow. At sunrise or sunset, when the light must follow a longer path through the Earth's atmosphere, the sun looks red (red having the longest wavelengths).

How long does it take **light from the sun** to reach the Earth?

Sunlight takes about eight minutes and 20 seconds to reach the Earth, traveling at 186,282 miles (299,792 kilometers) per second.

How long is a **solar cycle**?

The solar cycle is the periodic change in the number of sun spots. The cycle is taken as the interval between successive minima and is about 11.1 years. During an entire cycle, solar flares, sunspots, and other magnetic phenomena move from intense activity to relative calm and back again. The solar cycle is one area of study to be carried out by up to 10 ATLAS space missions designed to probe the chemistry and physics of the atmosphere. These studies of the solar cycle will yield a more detailed picture of the Earth's atmosphere and its response to changes in the sun.

What is the **sunspot cycle**?

It is the fluctuating number of sunspots on the sun during an 11-year period. The variation in the number of sunspots seems to correspond with the increase or decrease in the number of solar flares. An increased number of sunspots means an increased number of solar flares.

When do **solar eclipses** happen?

A solar eclipse occurs when the moon passes between the Earth and the sun and all three bodies are aligned in the same plane. When the moon completely blocks Earth's view of the sun and the umbra, or dark part of the moon's shadow, reaches the Earth, a total eclipse occurs. A total eclipse happens only along a narrow path 100 to 200 miles (160 to 320 kilometers) wide called the track of totality. Just before totality, the only parts of the sun that are visible are a few points of light called Baily's beads shining through valleys on the moon's surface. Sometimes, a last bright flash of sunlight is seen—the diamond ring effect. During totality, which averages 2.5 minutes, but may last up to 7.5 minutes, the sky is dark and stars and other planets are easily seen. The corona, the sun's outer atmosphere, is also visible.

If the moon does not appear large enough in the sky to completely cover the sun, it appears silhouetted against the sun with a ring of sunlight showing around it. This is an annular eclipse. Because the sun is not completely covered, its corona cannot be seen and although the sky may darken, it will not be dark enough to see the stars.

During a partial eclipse of the sun, the penumbra of the moon's shadow strikes the Earth. A partial eclipse can also be seen on either side of the track of totality of an annular or total eclipse. The moon will cover part of the sun and the sky will not darken noticeably during a partial eclipse.

What is the safest way to **view a solar eclipse**?

Punch a pinhole in an index card and hold it two to three feet in front of another index card. The eclipse can be viewed safely through the hole. Encase the index card contraption in a box, using aluminum foil with a pinhole, and you'll see a sharper image of the eclipse. You may also purchase special glasses with aluminized Mylar lenses. Damage to the retina can occur if the eclipse is viewed with other contraptions like photographic filters, exposed film, smoked glass, camera lenses, telescopes, or binoculars.

When will the **next total solar eclipse** be visible from the United States?

It will occur on August 21, 2017, sweeping a path 70 miles (113 kilometers) wide from Salem, Oregon to Charleston, South Carolina.

What is a **sun dog**?

A sun dog is also known as a mock sun, false sun, or the 22° parhelia. It is a bright spot of light that sometimes appears on either side of the sun at the same distance above the horizon as the sun, and is separated from the sun by an angle of 22°.

What is **solar wind**?

Solar wind is caused by the expansion of gases in the sun's outermost atmosphere, the corona. Because of the corona's extremely high temperature of 4,000,000°F **39**

(2,200,000°C), the gases heat up and their atoms start to collide. The atoms lose electrons and become electrically charged ions. These ions create the solar wind. Solar wind has a velocity of 310 miles (500 kilometers) per second, and its density is approximately 82 ions per cubic inch (five ions per cubic centimeter). Because the Earth is surrounded by strong magnetic forces, its magnetosphere, it is protected from the solar wind particles. In 1959, the Soviet spacecraft *Luna 2* acknowledged the existence of solar wind and made the first measurements of its properties.

PLANETS AND MOONS
See also: The Earth

How old is the **solar system**?

It is is currently believed to be 4.5 billion years old. The Earth and the rest of the solar system formed from an immense cloud of gas and dust. Gravity and rotational forces caused the cloud to flatten into a disc and much of the cloud's mass to drift into the

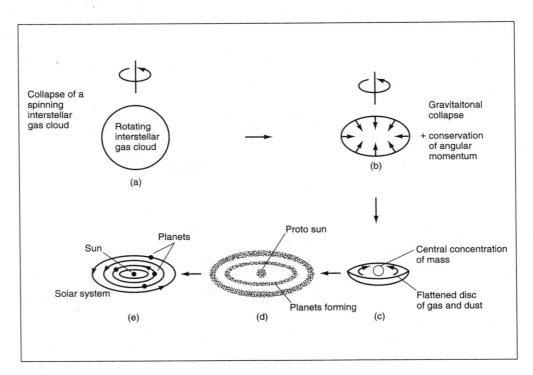

The evolution of the solar system from a gas cloud (a) to its present-day structure (e).

center. This material became the sun. The left-over parts of the cloud formed small bodies called planetesimals. These planetesimals collided with each other, gradually forming larger and larger bodies, some of which became the planets. This process is thought to have taken about 25 million years.

How **far are the planets** from the sun?

The planets revolve around the sun in elliptical orbits, with the sun at one focus of the ellipse. Thus, a planet is at times closer to the sun than at other times. The distances given below are the average distance from the sun, starting with Mercury, the planet closest to the sun, and moving outward.

Planet	Average distance	
	Miles	**Kilometers**
Mercury	35,983,000	57,909,100
Venus	67,237,700	108,208,600
Earth	92,955,900	149,598,000
Mars	141,634,800	227,939,200
Jupiter	483,612,200	778,298,400
Saturn	888,184,000	1,427,010,000
Uranus	1,782,000,000	2,869,600,000
Neptune	2,794,000,000	4,496,700,000
Pluto	3,666,000,000	5,913,490,000

How long do the planets take to go **around the sun**?

Planet	Period of revolution	
	Earth days	**Earth years**
Mercury	88	0.24
Venus	224.7	0.62
Earth	365.26	1.00
Mars	687	1.88
Jupiter	4,332.6	11.86
Saturn	10,759.2	29.46
Uranus	30,685.4	84.01
Neptune	60,189	164.8
Pluto	90,777.6	248.53

What are the **diameters** of the planets?

Planet	Diameter Miles	Kilometers
Mercury	3,031	4,878
Venus	7,520	12,104
Earth	7,926	12,756
Mars	4,221	6,794
Jupiter	88,846	142,984
Saturn	74,898	120,536
Uranus	31,763	51,118
Neptune	31,329	50,530
Pluto	1,423	2,290

Note: All diameters are as measured at the planet's equator.

What are the **colors** of the planets?

Planet	Color
Mercury	Orange
Venus	Yellow
Earth	Blue, brown, green
Mars	Red
Jupiter	Yellow, red, brown, white
Saturn	Yellow
Uranus	Green
Neptune	Blue
Pluto	Yellow

Which planets have **rings**?

Jupiter, Saturn, Uranus, and Neptune all have rings. Jupiter's rings were discovered by *Voyager 1* in March, 1979. The rings extend 80,240 miles (129,130 kilometers) from the center of the planet. They are about 4,300 miles (7,000 kilometers) in width and less than 20 miles (30 kilometers) thick. A faint inner ring is believed to extend to the edge of Jupiter's atmosphere.

Saturn has the largest, most spectacular set of rings in the solar system. That the planet is surrounded by a ring system was first recognized by the Dutch astronomer Christiaan Huygens (1629–1695) in 1659. Saturn's rings are 169,800 miles (273,200 kilometers) in diameter, but less than 10 miles (16 kilometers) thick. There are six different rings, the largest of which appear to be divided into thousands of ringlets. The rings appear to be composed of pieces of water ice ranging in size from tiny grains to blocks several tens of yards in diameter.

In 1977 when Uranus occulted (passed in front of) a star, scientists observed that the light from the star flickered or winked several times before the planet itself covered the star. The same flickering occurred in reverse order after the occultation. The reason for this was determined to be a ring around Uranus. Nine rings were initially identified, and *Voyager 2* observed two more in 1986. The rings are thin, narrow, and very dark.

Voyager 2 also discovered a series of at least four rings around Neptune in 1989. Some of the rings appear to have arcs, areas where there is a higher density of material than at other parts of the ring.

Who discovered **Saturn's rings**?

Unbeknownst to him, Galileo was probably the first to discover Saturn's rings in 1610. Because his telescope was small, Galileo could not see the rings properly and assumed they were satellites. In 1656, Christiaan Huygens discovered a ring around Saturn with a more powerful telescope. Later, in 1675, Jean Domenique Cassini distinguished two rings around Saturn. Still later, more rings were discovered and, as recently as 1980, ringlets were observed.

What is the **gravitational force** on each of the planets, the moon, and the sun relative to the Earth?

If the gravitational force on the Earth is taken as 1, the comparative forces are

Sun	27.9
Mercury	0.37
Venus	0.88
Earth	1.00
Moon	0.16
Mars	0.38
Jupiter	2.64
Saturn	1.15
Uranus	0.93
Neptune	1.22
Pluto	0.06

Weight comparisons can be made by using this table. If a person weighed 100 pounds (45.36 kilograms) on Earth, then the weight of the person on the Moon would be 16 pounds (7.26 kilograms) or 100×0.16.

Is **a day** the same on all the planets?

No. A day, the period of time it takes for a planet to make one complete turn on its axis, varies from planet to planet. Venus, Uranus, and Pluto display retrograde motion, that is to say, they rotate in the opposite direction from the other planets. The table below lists the length of the day for each planet.

Planet	Earth days	Length of day	
		Hours	Minutes
Mercury	58	15	30
Venus	243		32
Earth		23	56
Mars		24	37
Jupiter		9	50
Saturn		10	39
Uranus		17	14
Neptune		16	03
Pluto	6	09	18

Which planets are called **"inferior"** planets and which are **"superior"** planets?

An inferior planet is one whose orbit is nearer to the sun than Earth's orbit is. Mercury and Venus are the inferior planets. Superior planets are those whose orbits around the sun lie beyond that of Earth. Mars, Jupiter, Saturn, Uranus, Neptune, and Pluto are the superior planets. The terms have nothing to do with the quality of an individual planet.

What are the **Jovian** and **terrestrial** planets?

Jupiter, Saturn, Uranus, and Neptune are the Jovian (the adjectival form for the word "Jupiter"), or Jupiter-like, planets. They are giant planets, composed primarily of light elements such as hydrogen and helium.

Mercury, Venus, Earth, and Mars are the terrestrial (derived from "terra," the Latin word for "earth"), or Earth-like, planets. They are small in size, have solid surfaces, and are composed of rocks and iron. Pluto appears to be a terrestrial-type planet as well, but it may have a different origin from the other planets.

What is unique about the **rotation** of the planet **Venus**?

Unlike Earth and most of the other planets, Venus rotates in a retrograde, or opposite, direction with relation to its orbital motion about the sun. It rotates so slowly that

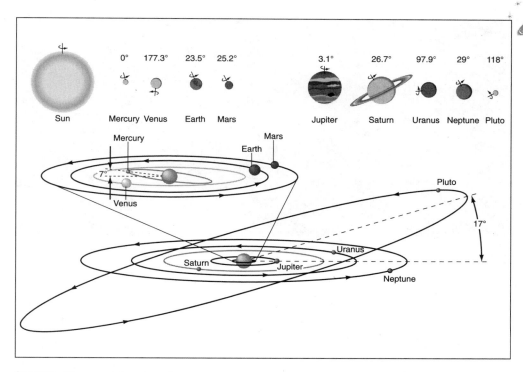

Schematic of the present-day solar system.

only two sunrises and sunsets occur each Venusian year. Uranus and Pluto's rotation are also retrograde.

Is it true that the **rotation speed of the Earth** varies?

The rotation speed is at its maximum in late July and early August and at its minimum in April; the difference in the length of the day is about 0.0012 second. Since about 1900 the Earth's rotation has been slowing at a rate of approximately 1.7 seconds per year. In the geologic past the Earth's rotational period was much faster; days were shorter and there were more days in the year. About 350 million years ago, the year had 400 to 410 days; 280 million years ago, a year was 390 days long.

Is it true that the **Earth is closer to the sun in winter** than in summer in the northern hemisphere?

Yes. However, the Earth's axis, the line around which the planet rotates, is tipped 23.5° with respect to the plane of revolution around the sun. When the Earth is closest to the sun (its perihelion, about January 3), the northern hemisphere is tilted away from

45

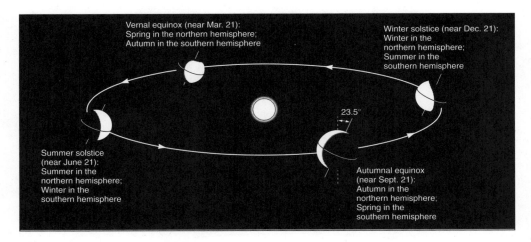

The seasons.

the sun. This causes winter in the northern hemisphere while the southern hemisphere is having summer. When the Earth is farthest from the sun (its aphelion, around July 4), the situation is reversed, with the northern hemisphere tilted towards the sun. At this time, it is summer in the northern hemisphere and winter in the southern hemisphere.

What is the **circumference of the Earth**?

The Earth is an oblate ellipsoid—a sphere slightly flattened at the poles and bulging at the equator. The distance around the Earth at the equator is 24,902 miles (40,075 kilometers). The distance around the Earth through the poles is 24,860 miles (40,008 kilometers).

What is the **precession** of the **equinoxes**?

The "precession of the equinoxes" is the 26,000-year circular movement of the Earth's axis. It is caused by the bulging at the equator, which makes the Earth's axis twist in such a way that the North and South Poles complete a circle every 26,000 years. Every year when the sun crosses the equator at the time of the equinox, it is in a slightly different position than the previous year. This movement proceeds eastward until a circle is completed.

Is there **life on Mars**?

Three experiments conducted on the composition of the Martian soil and atmosphere, carried out by the Viking Lander in July 1976, offered no evidence of life on Mars.

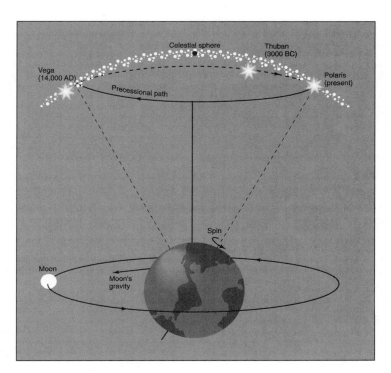

The precessional motion of the Earth.

Is it true that Pluto is not always the **outermost planet** in the solar system?

Pluto's very eccentric orbit carried it inside Neptune's orbit on January 23, 1979. It will remain there until March 15, 1999. During this time, Neptune is the outermost planet in the solar system. However, because they are so far apart, the planets are in no danger of colliding with one another.

Pluto, discovered in 1930 by American astronomer Clyde Tombaugh (b. 1906), is the smallest planet in the solar system. It is composed of rock and ice, with methane ice on the surface and a thin methane atmosphere. Pluto's single moon, Charon, discovered by James Christy in 1978, has a diameter of 741 miles (1,192 kilometers). This makes Charon, at half the size of Pluto, a very large moon relative to the planet. Some astronomers consider Pluto and Charon to be a double planet system.

What is **Planet X**?

Astronomers have observed perturbations, or disturbances, in the orbits of Uranus and Neptune since the discoveries of both planets. They speculated that Uranus and Neptune were being influenced by the gravity of another celestial body. Pluto, discovered in 1930, does not appear to be large enough to cause these disturbances. The existence of another planet, known as Planet X, orbiting beyond Pluto, has been proposed. As yet there have been no sightings of this tenth planet, but the search continues. There is a possibility that the unmanned space probes *Pioneer 10 & 11* and *Voyager 1 & 2*, now heading out of the solar system, will be able to locate this elusive object.

What does it mean when a **planet** is said to be in **opposition**?

A body in the solar system is in opposition when its longitude differs from the sun by 180°. In that position, it is exactly opposite the sun in the sky and it crosses the meridian at midnight.

How can an observer distinguish **planets** from **stars**?

In general, planets emit a constant light or shine, whereas stars appear to twinkle. The twinkling effect is caused by the combination of the distance between the stars and Earth and the refractive effect Earth's atmosphere has on a star's light. Planets are relatively closer to Earth than stars and their disk-like shapes average out the twinkling effect, except when they're observed near the Earth's horizon.

How many **moons** does each planet have?

Planet	Number of moons	Names of moons
Mercury	0	
Venus	0	
Earth	1	The Moon (sometimes called Luna)
Mars	2	Phobos, Deimos
Jupiter	16*	Metis, Adrastea, Amalthea, Thebe, Io, Europa, Ganymede, Callisto, Leda, Himalia, Lysithia, Elara, Ananke, Carme, Pasiphae, Sinope

Planet	Number of moons	Names of moons
Saturn	18*	Atlas, 1981S13 (unnamed as yet), Prometheus, Pandora, Epimetheus, Janus, Mimas, Enceladus, Tethys, Telesto, Calypso, Dione, Helene, Rhea, Titan, Hyperion, Iapetus, Phoebe
Uranus	15	Cordelia, Ophelia, Bianca, Cressida, Desdemona, Juliet, Portia, Rosalind, Belinda, Puck, Miranda, Ariel, Umbriel, Titania, Oberon
Neptune	8	Naiad, Thalassa, Despina, Galatea, Larissa, Proteus, Triton, Nereid
Pluto	1	Charon

*Several other satellites have been reported but not confirmed.

How far is the **moon** from the Earth?

Since the moon's orbit is elliptical, its distance varies from about 221,463 miles (356,334 kilometers) at perigee (closest approach to Earth), to 251,968 miles (405,503 kilometers) at apogee (farthest point), with the average distance being 238,857 miles (384,392 kilometers).

What are the **diameter** and **circumference** of the **moon**?

The moon's diameter is 2,159 miles (3,475 kilometers) and its circumference is 6,790 miles (10,864 kilometers). The moon is 27% the size of the Earth.

Why does the moon always keep the **same face toward the Earth**?

Only one side of the moon is seen because it always rotates in exactly the same length of time that it takes to revolve about the Earth. This combination of motions (called "captured rotation") means that it always keeps the same side toward the Earth.

What are the **phases** of the moon?

The phases of the moon are changes in the moon's appearance during the month, which are caused by the moon's turning different portions of its illuminated hemisphere towards the Earth. When the moon is between the Earth and the sun, its daylight side is turned away from the Earth, so it is not seen. This is called the new moon. As the moon continues its revolution around the Earth, more and more of its surface becomes visible. This is called the waxing crescent phase. About a week after the new moon, half the moon is visible—the first quarter phase. During the next week, more than half of the moon is seen; this is called the waxing gibbous phase. Finally, about

49

two weeks after the new moon, the moon and sun are on opposite sides of the Earth. The side of the moon facing the sun is also facing the Earth, and all the moon's illuminated side is seen as a full moon. In the next two weeks the moon goes through the same phases, but in reverse from a waning gibbous to third or last quarter to waning crescent phase. Gradually, less and less of the moon is visible until a new moon occurs again.

Is the moon really blue during a **blue moon**?

The term "blue moon," the second full moon in a single month, does not refer to the color of the moon. A blue moon occurs, on average, every 2.72 years. Since 29.53 days pass between full moons (a synodial month), there is never a blue moon in February. On rare occasions, a blue moon can be seen twice in one year, but only in certain parts of the world. The next pair of blue moons will occur in 1999, during the months of January and March.

A bluish-looking moon can result from effects of the Earth's atmosphere. For example, the phenomenon was widely observed in North America on September 26, 1950, due to Canadian forest fires that had scattered high-altitude dust.

What is the difference between a **hunter's moon** and a **harvest moon**?

The harvest moon is the full moon nearest the autumnal equinox (on or about September 23). It is followed by a period of several successive days when the moon rises soon after sunset. In the southern hemisphere the harvest moon is the full moon closest to the vernal equinox (on or about March 21). This gives farmers extra hours of light for harvesting crops. The next full moon after the harvest moon is called the hunter's moon.

Why do **lunar eclipses** happen?

A lunar eclipse occurs only during a full moon when the moon is on one side of the Earth, the sun is on the opposite side, and all three bodies are aligned in the same plane. In this alignment the Earth blocks the sun's rays to cast a shadow on the moon. In a total lunar eclipse the moon seems to disappear from the sky when the whole moon passes through the umbra, or total shadow, created by the Earth. A total lunar eclipse may last up to one hour and 40 minutes. If only part of the moon enters the umbra, a partial eclipse occurs. A penumbral eclipse takes place if all or part of the moon passes through the penumbra (partial shadow or "shade") without touching the umbra. It is difficult to detect this type of eclipse from Earth. From the moon one could see that the Earth blocked only part of the sun.

What is the **moon's tail** that astronomers have discovered?

A glowing 15,000 mile (24,000 kilometer) long tail of sodium atoms streams from the moon. The faint, orange glow of sodium cannot be seen by the naked eye but it is detectable by instruments. Astronomers are not certain of the source of these sodium atoms.

What are the **craters** on the moon that are named for the famous Curie family?

Curie—named for Pierre Curie (1859–1906), French chemist and Nobel prize winner.

Sklodowska—the maiden name of Marie Curie (1867–1934), French physical chemist and Nobel prize winner.

Joliot—named for physicist Frederic Joliot-Curie (1900–1958), Pierre and Marie's son-in-law and Nobel prize winner.

What is the **Genesis rock**?

The Genesis rock is a lunar rock brought to Earth by *Apollo 15*. It is approximately 4.15 billion years old, which is only 0.5 billion years younger than the generally accepted age of the moon.

COMETS, METEORITES, ETC.

Where are **asteroids** found?

The asteroids, also called the minor planets, are smaller than any of the nine major planets in the solar system and are not satellites of any major planet. The term asteroid means "starlike" because asteroids appear to be points of light when seen through a telescope.

Most asteroids are located between Mars and Jupiter, between 2.1 and 3.3 AUs (astronomical units) from the sun. Ceres, the largest and first to be discovered, was found by Giuseppe Piazzi on January 1, 1801, and has a diameter of 582 miles (936 kilometers). A second asteroid, Pallas, was discovered in 1802. Since then, astronomers have identified more than 18,000 asteroids and have established orbits for about 5,000 of them. Some of these have diameters of only 0.62 mile (one kilometer). Originally, astronomers thought the asteroids were remnants of a planet that had been destroyed; now they believe asteroids to be material that never became a planet, possibly because it was affected by Jupiter's strong gravity.

Not all asteroids are in this main asteroid belt. Three groups reside in the inner solar system. The Aten asteroids have orbits that lie primarily inside Earth's orbit. However, at their farthest point from the sun, these asteroids may cross Earth's orbit. The Apollo asteroids cross Earth's orbit; some come even closer than the moon. The Amor asteroids cross the orbit of Mars, and some come close to Earth's orbit. The Trojan asteroids move in virtually the same orbit as Jupiter but at points 60° ahead or 60° behind the planet. In 1977 Charles Kowal discovered an object now known as Chiron orbiting between Saturn and Uranus. Originally cataloged as an asteroid, Chiron was later observed to have a coma (a gaseous halo), and it may be reclassified as a comet.

An **asteroid** came close to hitting the Earth sometime in 1989. How much **damage** might it have done?

Asteroid 1989 FC passed within 434,000 miles (700,000 kilometers) of the Earth on March 22, 1989. The impact, had it hit the Earth, would have delivered the energy equivalent of more than one million tons of exploding TNT and created a crater up to 4.3 miles (seven kilometers) across.

What was the **Tunguska Event**?

On June 30, 1908, a violent explosion occurred in the atmosphere over the Podkamennaya Tunguska River, in a remote part of central Siberia. The blast's consequences were similar to an H-bomb going off, leveling thousands of square miles of forest. The shock of the explosion was heard more than 600 miles (960 kilometers) away. A number of theories have been proposed to account for this event.

Some people thought that a large meteorite or a piece of anti-matter had fallen to Earth. But a meteorite, composed of rock and metal, would have created a crater and none was found at the impact site. There are no high radiation levels in the area that would have resulted from the collision of anti-matter and matter. Two other theories include a mini–black hole striking the Earth or the crash of an extraterrestrial spaceship. However, a mini–black hole would have passed through the Earth and there is no record of a corresponding explosion on the other side of the world. As for the spaceship, no wreckage of such a craft was ever found.

The most likely cause of the explosion was the entry into the atmosphere of a piece of a comet, which would have produced a large fireball and blast wave. Since a comet is composed primarily of ice, the fragment would have melted during its passage through the Earth's atmosphere, leaving no impact crater and no debris. Since the Tunguska Event coincided with the Earth's passage through the orbit of Comet Encke, the explosion could have been caused by a piece of that comet.

From where do **comets** originate?

According to a theory developed by Dutch astronomer Jan Oort, there is a large cloud of gas, dust, and comets orbiting beyond Pluto out to perhaps 100,000 astronomical units (AU). Occasional stars passing close to this cloud disturb some of the comets from their orbits. Some fall inwards towards the sun.

Comets, sometimes called "dirty snowballs," are made up mostly of ice, with some dust mixed in. When a comet moves closer to the sun, the dust and ice of the core, or nucleus, heats up, producing a tail of material that trails along behind it. The tail is pushed out by the solar wind and almost always points away from the sun.

Most comets have highly elliptical orbits that carry them around the sun and then fling them back out to the outer reaches of the solar system, never to return. Occasionally, however, a close passage by a comet near one of the planets can alter a comet's orbit, making it stay in the middle or inner solar system. Such a comet is called a short-period comet because it passes close to the sun at regular intervals. The most famous short-period comet is Comet Halley, which reaches perihelion (the point in its orbit that is closest to the sun) about every 76 years. Comet Encke, with an orbital period of 3.3 years, is another short-period comet.

When will **Halley's comet** return?

Halley's comet returns about every 76 years. It was most recently seen in 1985/1986 and is predicted to appear again in 2061, then in 2134. Every appearance of what is now known as Comet Halley has been noted by astronomers since the year 239 B.C.

Edmund Halley.

The comet is named for Edmund Halley (1656–1742), England's second Astronomer Royal. In 1682 he observed a bright comet and noted that it was moving in an orbit similar to comets seen in 1531 and 1607. He concluded that the three comets were actually one and the same and that the comet had an orbit of 76 years. In 1705 Halley published *A Synopsis of the Astronomy of Comets*, in which he predicted that the comet seen in 1531, 1607, and 1682 would return in 1758. On Christmas night, 1758, a German farmer and amateur astronomer named Johann Palitzsch spotted the comet in just the area of the sky that Halley had foretold.

Prior to Halley, comets appeared at irregular intervals and were often thought to

53

be harbingers of disaster and signs of divine wrath. Halley proved that they are natural objects subject to the laws of gravity.

What is comet Hale-Bopp?

Named after Alan Hale and Thomas Bopp, Hale-Bopp was discovered on July 23, 1995. It will be visible by August 1996, and will be at its brightest during March and April of 1997.

When do meteor showers occur?

There are a number of groups of meteoroids orbiting the sun just as the Earth is. When Earth's orbit intercepts the path of one of these swarms of meteoroids, some of them enter Earth's atmosphere. When friction with the air causes a meteoroid to burn up, the streak, or shooting star, that is produced is called a meteor. Large numbers of meteors can produce a spectacular shower of light in the night sky. Meteor showers are named for the constellation that occupies the area of the sky from which they originate. Listed below are 10 meteor showers and the dates during the year during which they can be seen.

Name of Shower	Dates
Quadrantids	January 1–6
Lyrids	April 19–24
Eta Aquarids	May 1–8
Perseids	July 25–August 18
Orionids	October 16–26
Taurids	October 20–November 20
Leonids	November 13–17
Phoenicids	December 4–5
Geminids	December 7–15
Ursids	December 17–24

How does a meteorite differ from a meteoroid?

A meteorite is a natural object of extraterrestrial origin that survives passage through the Earth's atmosphere and hits the Earth's surface. A meteorite is often confused with a meteoroid or a meteor. A meteoroid is a small object in outer space, generally less than 30 feet (10 meters) in diameter. A meteor (sometimes called a shooting star) is the flash of light seen when an object passes through Earth's atmosphere and burns as a result of heating caused by friction. A meteoroid becomes a meteor when it enters the Earth's atmosphere; if any portion of a meteoroid lands on Earth, it is a meteorite.

There are three kinds of meteorites. Irons contain 85% to 95% iron; the rest of their mass is mostly nickel. Stony irons are relatively rare meteorites composed of about 50% iron and 50% silicates. Stones are made up mostly of silicates and other stony materials.

How many meteorites land on the Earth in a given year?

Approximately 26,000 meteorites, each weighing over 3.5 ounces (99.2 grams) land on the Earth during a given year. This figure is compiled from the number of fireballs visually observed by the Canadian Camera Network. Of that number, only five or six falls are witnessed or cause property damage. The majority fall in the oceans, covering over 70% of the Earth's surface.

What are the largest meteorites that have been found in the world?

The famous Willamette (Oregon) iron, displayed at the American Museum of Natural History in New York, is the largest specimen found in the United States. It is 10 feet (3.048 meters) long and five feet (1.524 meters) high.

Name	Location	Weight	
		Tons	Tonnes
Hoba West	Namibia	66.1	60
Ahnighito (The Tent)	Greenland	33.5	30.4
Bacuberito	Mexico	29.8	27
Mbosi	Tanzania	28.7	26
Agpalik	Greenland	22.2	20.1
Armanty	Outer Mongolia	22	20
Willamette	Oregon, USA	15.4	14
Chupaderos	Mexico	15.4	14
Campo del Cielo	Argentina	14.3	13
Mundrabilla	Western Australia	13.2	12
Morito	Mexico	12.1	11

How do scientists know that some meteorites that were found in Antarctica came from the Moon?

Because of the high-quality reference collection of lunar rocks collected during space-flights to the moon, the original 1979 meteorite find in Antarctica and the 10 subsequent findings were varified as lunar in origin.

OBSERVATION AND MEASUREMENT

Who is considered the founder of systematic astronomy?

The Greek scientist Hipparchus (fl. 146–127 B.C.E.) is considered to be the father of systematic astronomy. He measured as accurately as possible the directions of objects in the sky. He compiled the first catalog of stars, containing about 850 entries, and designated each star's celestial coordinates, indicating its position in the sky. Hipparchus also divided the stars according to their apparent brightness or magnitudes.

What is a light year?

A light year is a measure of distance, not time. It is the distance that light, which travels in a vacuum at the rate of 186,282 miles (299,792 kilometers) per second, can travel in a year (365.25 days). This is equal to 5.87 trillion miles (9.46 trillion kilometers).

Besides the light year, what other units are used to measure distances in astronomy?

The astronomical unit (AU) is often used to measure distances within the solar system. One AU is equal to the average distance between the Earth and the sun, or 92,955,630 miles (149,597,870 kilometers). The parsec is equal to 3.26 light years, or about 19.18 trillion miles (30.82 trillion kilometers).

How are new celestial objects named?

Many stars and planets have names that date back to antiquity. The International Astronomical Union (IAU), the professional astronomers organization, has attempted, in this century, to standardize names given to newly discovered celestial objects and their surface features.

Stars are generally called by their traditional names, most of which are of Greek, Roman, or Arabic origin. They are also identified by the constellation in which they appear, designated in order of brightness by Greek letters. Thus Sirius is also called alpha Canis Majoris, which means it is the brightest star in the constellation Canis Major. Other stars are called by catalog numbers, which include the star's coordinates. To the horror of many astronomers, several commercial star registries exist, and for a fee, you can submit a star name to them. These names are not officially recognized by the IAU.

The IAU has made some recommendations for naming the surface features of the planets and their satellites. For example, features on Mercury are named for com-

What is widely considered to be one of the earliest celestial observatories?

Built in England over a period of years between 2500 and 1700 B.C.E., Stonehenge is one of the earliest observatories or observatory-temples. It is widely believed that its primary function was to observe the mid-summer and mid-winter solstices.

posers, poets, and writers; features of Venus for women; and features on Saturn's moon Mimas for people and places in Arthurian legend.

Comets are named for their discoverers. Newly discovered asteroids are first given a temporary designation consisting of the year of discovery plus two letters. The first letter indicates the half month of discovery and the second the order of discovery in that half month. Thus asteroid 1991BA was the first asteroid (A) discovered in the second half of January (B) in 1991. After an asteroid's orbit is determined it is given a permanent number and its discoverer is given the honor of naming it. Asteroids have been named after such diverse things as mythological figures (Ceres, Vesta), an airline (Swissair), and the Beatles (Lennon, McCartney, Harrison, Starr).

What is an **astrolabe**?

Invented by the Greeks or Alexandrians in about 100 B.C.E. or before, an astrolabe is a two-dimensional working model of the heavens, with sights for observations. It consists of two concentric flat disks, one fixed, representing the observer on Earth, the other moving, which can be rotated to represent the appearance of the celestial sphere at a given moment. Given latitude, date, and time, the observer can read off the altitude and azimuth of the sun, the brightest stars, and the planets. By measuring the altitude of a particular body, one can find the time. The astrolabe can also be used to find times of sunrise, sunset, twilight, or the height of a tower or depth of a well. It was replaced by the sextant and other more accurate instruments.

Who invented the **telescope**?

Hans Lippershey (ca. 1570–1619), a German-Dutch lens grinder and spectacle maker, is generally credited with inventing the telescope in 1608 because he was the first scientist to apply for a patent. Two other inventors, Zacharias Janssen and Jacob Metius, also developed telescopes. Modern historians consider Lippershey and Janssen as the two likely candidates for the title of inventor of the telescope, with Lippershey possessing the strongest claim. Lippershey used his telescope for observing grounded objects from a distance.

In 1609, Galileo also developed his own refractor telescope for astronomical studies. Although small by today's standards, the telescope enabled Galileo to observe the Milky Way and to identify blemishes on the moon's surface as craters.

Who is the **Hubble** for whom the **space telescope** is named?

Edwin Powell Hubble (1889–1953) was an American astronomer known for his studies of galaxies. His study of nebulae, or clouds—the faint, unresolved luminous patches in the sky—showed that some of them were large groups of many stars. Hubble classified galaxies by their shapes as being spiral, elliptical, or irregular.

Hubble's Law establishes a relationship between the velocity of recession of a galaxy and its distance. The speed at which a galaxy is moving away from our solar system (measured by its redshift, the shift of its light to longer wavelengths, presumed to be caused by the Doppler effect) is directly proportional to the galaxy's distance from it.

The Hubble Space Telescope was deployed by the space shuttle *Discovery* on April 25, 1990. The telescope, which would be free of distortions caused by the Earth's atmosphere, was designed to see deeper into space than any telescope on land. However, on June 27, 1990, the National Aeronautics and Space Administration announced that the telescope had a defect in one of its mirrors that prevented it from properly focusing. Although other instruments, including one designed to make observations in ultraviolet light, were still operating, nearly 40% of the telescope's experiments had to be postponed until repairs were made. On December 2, 1993, astronauts were able to make the necessary repairs. Four of Hubble's six gyroscopes were replaced as well as two solar panels. Hubble's primary camera, which had a flawed mirror, was also replaced.

EXPLORATION

How probable is it that **intelligent life** exists on other planets?

The possibility of intelligent life depends on several factors. An estimation can be calculated by using an equation developed originally by American astronomer Frank Drake (b. 1930). Drake's equation reads $N = N_* f_p n_e f_l f_i f_c f_L$. This means that the number of advanced civilizations (N) is equal to

Is anyone looking for extraterrestrial life?

A program called SETI (the Search for Extraterrestrial Intelligence) began in 1960, when American astronomer Frank Drake (b. 1930) spent three months at the National Radio Astronomy Observatory in Green Bank, West Virginia, searching for radio signals coming from the nearby stars Tau Ceti and Epsilon Eridani. Although no signals were detected and scientists interested in SETI have often been ridiculed, support for the idea of seeking out intelligent life in the universe has grown.

Project Sentinel, which used a radio dish at Harvard University's Oak Ridge Observatory in Massachusetts, could monitor 128,000 channels at a time. This project was upgraded in 1985 to META (Megachannel Extraterrestrial Assay), thanks in part to a donation by filmmaker Steven Spielberg. Project META is capable of receiving 8.4 million channels. NASA began a 10-year search in 1992 using radio telescopes in Arecibo, Puerto Rico, and Barstow, California.

Scientists are searching for radio signals that stand out from the random noises caused by natural objects. Such signals might repeat at regular intervals or contain mathematical sequences. There are millions of radio channels and a lot of sky to be examined and, as of October 1995, Project BETA (Billion-channel Extraterrestrial Assay) has been scanning a quarter of a billion channels. This new design improves upon Project META 300-fold, making the challenge of scanning millions of radio channels seem less daunting.

N_*, the number of stars in the Milky Way galaxy, times

f_p, the fraction of those stars that have planets, times

n_e, the number of planets capable of supporting life, times

f_l, the fraction of planets suitable for life on which life actually arises, times

f_i, the fraction of planets where intelligent life evolves, times

f_c, the fraction of planets with intelligent life that develops a technically advanced civilization, times

f_L, the fraction of time that a technical civilization lasts.

The equation is obviously subjective and the answer depends on whether optimistic or pessimistic numbers are assigned to the various factors. However, the galaxy is so large that the possibility of life elsewhere cannot be ruled out.

What is meant by the phrase "greening of the galaxy"?

The expression means the spreading of human life, technology, and culture through interstellar space and eventually across the entire Milky Way galaxy, the Earth's home galaxy.

When was the Outer Space Treaty signed?

The United Nations Outer Space Treaty was signed on January 23, 1967. The treaty provides a framework for the exploration and sharing of outer space. It governs the outer space activities of nations that wish to exploit and make use of space, the moon, and other celestial bodies. It is based on a humanist and pacifist philosophy and on the principle of the nonappropriation of space and the freedom that all nations have to explore and use space. A very large number of countries have signed this agreement, including those from the Western alliance, the former Eastern bloc, and non-aligned countries.

Space law, or those rules governing the space activities of various countries, international organizations, and private industries, has been evolving since 1957 when the General Assembly of the United Nations created the Committee on the Peaceful Uses of Outer Space (COPUOS). One of its subcommittees was instrumental in drawing up the 1967 Outer Space Treaty.

What is a "close encounter of the third kind"?

UFO expert J. Allen Hynek (1910–1986) developed the following scale to describe encounters with extraterrestrial beings or vessels:

Close Encounter of the First Kind—sighting of a UFO at close range with no other physical evidence.

Close Encounter of the Second Kind—sighting of a UFO at close range, but with some kind of proof, such as a photograph, or an artifact from a UFO.

Close Encounter of the Third Kind—sighting of an actual extraterrestrial being.

Close Encounter of the Fourth Kind—abduction by an extraterrestrial spacecraft.

Who was the first man in space?

Yuri Gagarin (1934–1968), a Soviet cosmonaut, became the first man in space when he made a full orbit of the Earth in *Vostok I* on April 12, 1961. Gagarin's flight lasted only one hour and 48 minutes, but as the first man in space, he became an international hero. Partly because of this Soviet success, U.S. President John F. Kennedy (1917–1963) announced on May 25, 1961, that the United States would land a man on the moon before the end of the decade. The United States took its first step toward that goal when it launched the first American into orbit on February 20, 1962. Astronaut John H. Glenn Jr. (b. 1921) completed three orbits in *Friendship 7* and traveled about 81,000 miles (130,329 kilometers). Prior to this, on May 5, 1961, Alan B. Shepard Jr. (b. 1923) became the first American to pilot a spaceflight, aboard *Freedom 7*. This suborbital flight reached an altitude of 116.5 miles (187.45 kilometers).

What did NASA mean when it said *Voyager 1* and *2* would take a "grand tour" of the planets?

Once every 176 years the giant outer planets—Jupiter, Saturn, Uranus, and Neptune—align themselves in such a pattern that a spacecraft launched from Earth to Jupiter at just the right time might be able to visit the other three planets on the same mission. A technique called "gravity assist" used each planet's gravity as a power boost to point *Voyager* toward the next planet. 1977 was the opportune year for the "grand tour."

What is the **message** attached to the *Voyager* spacecraft?

Voyager 1 (launched September 5, 1977) and *Voyager 2* (launched August 20, 1977) were unmanned space probes designed to explore the outer planets and then travel out of the solar system. A gold-coated copper phonograph record containing a message to any possible extraterrestrial civilization that they may encounter is attached to each spacecraft. The record contains both video and audio images of Earth and the civilization that sent this message to the stars.

The record begins with 118 pictures. These show the Earth's position in the galaxy; a key to the mathematical notation used in other pictures; the sun; other planets in the solar system; human anatomy and reproduction; various types of terrain (seashore, desert, mountains); examples of vegetation and animal life; people of both sexes and of all ages and ethnic types engaged in a number of activities; structures (from grass huts to the Taj Mahal to the Sydney Opera House) showing diverse architectural styles; and means of transportation, including roads, bridges, cars, planes, and space vehicles.

The pictures are followed by greetings from Jimmy Carter, then president of the United States, and Kurt Waldheim, then Secretary General of the United Nations. Brief messages in 54 languages, ranging from ancient Sumerian to English, are included, as is a "song" of the humpback whales.

61

The next section is a series of sounds common to the Earth. These include thunder, rain, wind, fire, barking dogs, footsteps, laughter, human speech, the cry of an infant, and the sounds of a human heartbeat and human brainwaves.

The record concludes with approximately 90 minutes of music, "Earth's Greatest Hits." These musical selections were drawn from a broad spectrum of cultures and include such diverse pieces as a Pygmy girl's initiation song; bagpipe music from Azerbaijan; the Fifth Symphony, First Movement by Ludwig von Beethoven; and "Johnny B. Goode" by Chuck Berry.

It will be tens, or even hundreds of thousands of years before either *Voyager* comes close to another star, and perhaps the message will never be heard; but it is a sign of humanity's hope to encounter life elsewhere in the universe.

Which astronauts have **walked on the moon**?

Twelve astronauts have walked on the moon. Each Apollo flight had a crew of three. One crew member remained in orbit in the command service module (CSM) while the other two actually landed on the moon.

Apollo 11, July 16–24, 1969
   Neil A. Armstrong
   Edwin E. Aldrin, Jr.
   Michael Collins (CSM pilot, did not walk on the moon)

Apollo 12, November 14–24, 1969
   Charles P. Conrad
   Alan L. Bean
   Richard F. Gordon, Jr. (CSM pilot, did not walk on the moon)

Apollo 14, January 31–February 9, 1971
   Alan B. Shepard, Jr.
   Edgar D. Mitchell
   Stuart A. Roosa (CSM pilot, did not walk on the moon)

Apollo 15, July 26–August 7, 1971
   David R. Scott
   James B. Irwin
   Alfred M. Worden (CSM pilot, did not walk on the moon)

Apollo 16, April 16–27, 1972
   John W. Young
   Charles M. Duke, Jr.
   Thomas K. Mattingly, II (CSM pilot, did not walk on the moon)

Apollo 17, December 7–19, 1972
   Eugene A. Cernan
   Harrison H. Schmitt
Ronald E. Evans (CSM pilot, did not walk on the moon)

Who made the first golf shot on the moon?

Alan B. Shepard Jr. (b. 1923), commander of *Apollo 14*, launched on January 31, 1971, made the first golf shot. He attached a six iron to the handle of the contingency sample return container, dropped a golf ball on the moon, and took a couple of one-handed swings. He missed with the first, but connected with the second. The ball, he reported, sailed for miles and miles.

Which **manned space flight** was the longest?

Dr. Valerij Polyakov manned a flight to the space station *Mir* on January 8, 1994. He returned aboard *Soyuz TM-20* on March 22, 1995, making the total time in space equal 438 days and 18 hours.

When and what was the **first animal** sent into orbit?

A dog named Laika, aboard the Soviet *Sputnik 2*, launched November 3, 1957, was the first animal sent into orbit. This event followed the successful Soviet launch on October 4, 1957, of *Sputnik 1*, the first man-made satellite ever placed in orbit. Laika was a very small female dog and became the first living creature to go into orbit. She was placed in a pressurized compartment within a capsule that weighed 1,103 pounds (500 kilograms). After a few days in orbit, she died, and *Sputnik 2* reentered the Earth's atmosphere on April 14, 1958. Some sources list the dog as a Russian samoyed laika named "Kudyavka" or "Limonchik."

What were the **first monkeys** and **chimpanzees** in space?

On a United States *Jupiter* flight on December 12, 1958, a squirrel monkey named Old Reliable was sent into space, but not into orbit. The monkey drowned during recovery.

On another *Jupiter* flight, on May 28, 1959, two female monkeys were sent 300 miles (482.7 kilometers) high. Able was a six-pound (2.7-kilogram) rhesus monkey and Baker was an 11-ounce (0.3-kilogram) squirrel monkey. Both were recovered alive.

A chimpanzee named Ham was used on a *Mercury* flight on January 31, 1961. Ham was launched to a height of 157 miles (253 kilometers) into space but did not go into orbit. His capsule reached a maximum speed of 5,857 miles (9,426 kilometers) per hour and landed 422 miles (679 kilometers) downrange in the Atlantic Ocean where he was recovered unharmed.

On November 29, 1961, the United States placed a chimpanzee named Enos into orbit and recovered him alive after two complete orbits around the Earth. Like the Soviets, who usually used dogs, the United States had to obtain information on the effects of space flight on living beings before they could actually launch a human into space.

Who were the first man and woman to **walk in space**?

On March 18, 1965, the Soviet cosmonaut Alexei Leonov (b. 1934) became the first person to walk in space when he spent 10 minutes outside his *Voskhod 2* spacecraft. The first woman to walk in space was Soviet cosmonaut Svetlana Savitskaya (b. 1947) who, during her second flight aboard the *Soyuz T-12* (July 17, 1984), performed 3½ hours of extravehicular activity.

The first American to walk in space was Edward White II (1930–1967) from the spacecraft *Gemini 4* on June 3, 1965. Kathryn D. Sullivan (b. 1951) became the first American woman to walk in space when she spent 3.5 hours outside the *Challenger* orbiter during the space shuttle mission 41G on October 11, 1984.

American astronaut Bruce McCandless II (b. 1937) performed the first untethered space walk from the space shuttle *Challenger* on February 7, 1984, using an MMU (manual maneuvering unit) backpack.

What were the **first words spoken** by an astronaut after touchdown of the lunar module on the *Apollo 11* flight, and by an astronaut standing on the moon?

On July 20, 1969, at 4:17:43 p.m. Eastern Daylight Time (20:17:43 Greenwich Mean Time), Neil A. Armstrong (b. 1930) and Edwin E. Aldrin Jr. (b. 1930) landed the lunar module *Eagle* in the moon's Sea of Tranquility, and Armstrong radioed: "Houston, Tranquility Base here. The *Eagle* has landed." Several hours later, when Armstrong descended the lunar module ladder and made the small jump between the *Eagle* and the lunar surface, he announced: "That's one small step for man, one giant leap for mankind." The article "a" was missing in the live voice transmission, and was later inserted in the record to amend the message to "one small step for *a* man."

What material was used in the **United States flag** planted on the moon by astronauts Neil Armstrong and Edwin Aldrin Jr.?

The astronauts erected a three-by-five foot nylon U.S. flag, its top edge braced by a spring wire to keep it extended.

What was the **first meal on the moon**?

American astronauts Neil A. Armstrong (b. 1930) and Edwin E. Aldrin, Jr. (b. 1930) ate four bacon squares, three sugar cookies, peaches, pineapple-grapefruit drink, and coffee before their historic moonwalk on July 20, 1969.

Who was the first **woman in space**?

Valentina V. Tereshkova-Nikolaeva (b. 1937), a Soviet cosmonaut, was the first woman in space. She was aboard the *Vostok 6*, launched June 16, 1963. She spent three days circling the Earth, completing 48 orbits. Although she had little cosmonaut training, she was an accomplished parachutist and was especially fit for the rigors of space travel.

The United States space program did not put a woman in space until 20 years later when, on June 18, 1983, Sally K. Ride (b. 1951) flew aboard the space shuttle *Challenger* mission STS-7. In 1987, she moved to the administrative side of NASA and was instrumental in issuing the "Ride Report," which recommended future missions and direction for NASA. She retired from NASA in August 1987 to become a research fellow at Stanford University after serving on the Presidential Commission that investigated the *Challenger* disaster. At present, she is the director of the California Space Institute at the University of California San Diego.

Sally Ride with fellow crewmembers.

What are some of the accomplishments of female astronauts?

First American woman in space: Sally K. Ride—June 18, 1983, aboard *Challenger* STS-7.

First American woman to walk in space: Kathryn D. Sullivan—October 11, 1984, aboard *Challenger* STS 41G.

First woman to make three spaceflights: Shannoin W. Lucid—June 17, 1985; October 18, 1989; and August 2, 1991.

First African American woman in space: Mae Carol Jemison—September 12, 1992, aboard *Endeavour*.

First American woman space shuttle pilot: Eileen M. Collins—February 3, 1995, aboard *Discovery*.

Who was the first **African American in space**?

Guion S. Bluford, Jr. (b. 1942), became the first African American to fly in space during the Space Shuttle *Challenger* mission STS-8 (August 30–September 5, 1983). Astronaut Bluford, who holds a Ph.D. in aerospace engineering, made a second shuttle flight aboard *Challenger* mission STS-61-A/Spacelab D1 (October 30–November 6, 1985). The first black man to fly in space was Cuban cosmonaut Arnaldo Tamayo-Mendez, who was aboard *Soyuz 38* and spent eight days aboard the Soviet space station *Salyut 6* during September 1980. Dr. Mae C. Jemison became the first African American woman in space on September 12, 1992 aboard the Space Shuttle *Endeavour* mission Spacelab-J.

Who were the first **married couple** to go into space together?

Astronauts Jan Davis and Mark Lee were the first married couple in space. They flew aboard the space shuttle *Endeavor* on an eight-day mission that began on September 12, 1992. Ordinarily NASA bars married couples from flying together. An exception was made for Davis and Lee because they had no children and had begun training for the mission long before they got married.

Who has spent the **most time in space**?

As of December 31, 1994, cosmonaut Musa H. Manarov had accumulated the most time in space. During two spaceflights—from December 21, 1987 to December 21, 1988, and from December 2, 1990 to May 26, 1991—Manarov clocked a total of 541 days in space.

How many successful space flights were **launched in 1991,** and by what countries?

A total of 88 flights that achieved Earth orbit or beyond were made in 1991:

Country or Organization	Number of Launches
U.S.S.R.	59
United States	18
European Space Agency	8
Japan	2
Peoples' Republic of China	1

In 1990, there were 116 such launches, with 75 by the former U.S.S.R.; 27 (including seven commercial launches) by the United States; five by the European Space Agency; five by the People's Republic of China; and one by Israel.

When was the first United States **satellite** launched?

Explorer 1, launched January 31, 1958, by the U.S. Army, was the first United States satellite launched into orbit. This 31-pound (14.06-kilogram) satellite carried instrumentation that led to the discovery of the Earth's radiation belts, which would be named after University of Iowa scientist James A. Van Allen. It followed four months after the launching of the world's first satellite, the Soviet Union's *Sputnik 1*. On October 3, 1957, the Soviet Union placed the large 184-pound (83.5-kilogram) satellite into low Earth orbit. It carried instrumentation to study the density and temperature of the upper atmosphere, and its launch was the event that opened the age of space.

What is the mission of the *Galileo* spacecraft?

Galileo, launched October 18, 1989, required almost six years to reach Jupiter after looping past Venus once and the Earth twice. The *Galileo* spacecraft was designed to make a detailed study of Jupiter and its rings and moons over a period of years. On December 7, 1995, it released a probe to analyze the different layers of Jupiter's atmosphere. *Galileo* will record a multitude of measurements of the planet, its four largest moons, and its mammoth magnetic field. The mission is scheduled to continue until the end of 1997.

Who was the founder of the **Soviet space program**?

Sergei P. Korolev (1907–1966) made enormous contributions to the development of Soviet manned space flight, and his name is linked with their most significant space achievements. Trained as an aeronautical engineer, he directed the Moscow group studying the principles of rocket propulsion, and in 1946 took over the Soviet program to develop long-range ballistic rockets. Under Korolev, the Soviets used these rockets for space projects and launched the world's first satellite in October 4, 1957. Besides a vigorous unmanned interplanetary research program, Korolev's goal was to place men in space, and following tests with animals his manned space flight program was initiated when Yuri Gagarin (1934–1968) was successfully launched into Earth's orbit.

How many **fatalities** have occurred during space-related missions?

The 14 astronauts and cosmonauts listed below died in space-related accidents.

Date	Astronaut/Cosmonaut	Mission
January 27, 1967	Roger Chaffee (U.S.)	Apollo 1
January 27, 1967	Edward White II (U.S.)	Apollo 1
January 27, 1967	Virgil "Gus" Grissom (U.S.)	Apollo 1
April 24, 1967	Vladimir Komarov (U.S.S.R.)	Soyuz 1
June 29, 1971	Viktor Patsayev (U.S.S.R.)	Soyuz 11
June 29, 1971	Vladislav Volkov (U.S.S.R.)	Soyuz 11
June 29, 1971	Georgi Dobrovolsky (U.S.S.R.)	Soyuz 11
January 28, 1986	Gregory Jarvis (U.S.)	STS 51L
January 28, 1986	Christa McAuliffe (U.S.)	STS 51L
January 28, 1986	Ronald McNair (U.S.)	STS 51L
January 28, 1986	Ellison Onizuka (U.S.)	STS 51L
January 28, 1986	Judith Resnik (U.S.)	STS 51L
January 28, 1986	Francis Scobee (U.S.)	STS 51L
January 28, 1986	Michael Smith (U.S.)	STS 51L

Chaffee, Grissom, and White died in a cabin fire during a test firing of the *Apollo 1* rocket. Komarov was killed in *Soyuz 1* when the capsule's parachute failed. Dobrovolsky, Patsayev, and Volkov were killed during the *Soyuz II*'s re-entry when a valve accidently opened and released their capsule's atmosphere. Jarvis, McAuliffe, McNair, Onizuka, Resnik, Scobee, and Smith died when the space shuttle *Challenger* STS 51L exploded 73 seconds after lift-off.

In addition, 19 other astronauts and cosmonauts have died of non-space related causes. Fourteen of these died in air crashes, four died of natural causes, and one died in an auto crash.

What was the **worst disaster** in the U.S. space program and what caused it?

Challenger mission STS 51L was launched on January 28, 1986, but exploded 73 seconds after lift-off. The entire crew of seven was killed and the *Challenger* was completely destroyed. The investigation of the *Challenger* tragedy was performed by the Rogers Commission, established and named for its chairman, former Secretary of State William Rogers.

The consensus of the Rogers Commission (which studied the accident for several months) and participating investigative agencies is that the accident was caused by a failure in the joint between the two lower segments of the right solid rocket motor. The specific failure was the destruction of the seals that are intended to prevent hot gases from leaking through the joint during the propellant burn of the rocket motor. The evidence assembled by the commission indicated that no other element of the space shuttle system contributed to this failure.

Although the commission did not affix blame to any individuals, the public record made clear that the launch should not have been made that day. The weather was unusually cold at Cape Canaveral and temperatures had dipped below freezing during the night. Test data had suggested that the seals (called O-rings) around the solid rocket booster joints lost much of their effectiveness in very cold weather.

What were some of the accomplishments of the **first nine *Challenger* spaceflights**?

First American woman in space—Sally Ride

First African American man in space—Guion S. Bluford Jr.

First American woman to spacewalk—Kathryn Sullivan

First shuttle spacewalk—Donald Peterson and Story Musgrave

First untethered spacewalk—Robert Stewart and Bruce McCandless

First satellite repair in orbit—Pinky Nelson and Ox Van Hoften

First Coke and Pepsi in orbit—1985

What is the composition of the **tiles** on the **underside of the space shuttle** and how hot do they get?

The 20,000 tiles are composed of a low-density, high purity silica fiber insulator hardened by ceramic bonding. Bonded to a Nomex fiber felt pad, each tile is directly bonded to the shuttle exterior. The maximum surface temperature can reach up to 922K to 978K (649°C to 704°C or 1,200°F to 1,300°F).

EARTH

AIR

See also: Climate and Weather

What is the **composition** of the **Earth's atmosphere**?

The Earth's atmosphere, apart from water vapor and pollutants, is composed of 78% nitrogen, 21% oxygen, and less than 1% each of argon and carbon dioxide. There are also traces of hydrogen, neon, helium, krypton, xenon, methane, and ozone. The Earth's original atmosphere was probably composed of ammonia and methane; 20 million years ago the air started to contain a broader variety of elements.

How many **layers** does the **Earth's atmosphere** contain?

The atmosphere, the "skin" of gas that surrounds the Earth, consists of five layers that are differentiated by temperature:

The troposphere is the lowest level; it averages about seven miles (11 kilometers) in thickness, varying from five miles (eight kilometers) at the poles to 10 miles (16 kilometers) at the equator. Most clouds and weather form in this layer. Temperature decreases with altitude in the troposphere.

The stratosphere ranges between seven and 30 miles (11 to 48 kilometers) above the Earth's surface. The ozone layer, important because it absorbs most of the sun's harmful ultraviolet radiation, is located in this band. Temperatures rise slightly with altitude to a maximum of about 32°F (0°C).

The mesosphere (above the stratosphere) extends from 30 to 55 miles (48 to 85 kilometers) above the Earth. Temperatures decrease with altitude to -130°F (-90°C).

71

The thermosphere (also known as the hetereosphere) is between 55 to 435 miles (85 to 700 kilometers). Temperatures in this layer range to 2696°F (1475°C).

The exosphere beyond the thermosphere, applies to anything above 435 miles (700 kilometers). In this layer, temperature no longer has any meaning.

The ionosphere is a region of the atmosphere that overlaps the others, reaching from 30 to 250 miles (48 to 402 kilometers). In this region, the air becomes ionized (electrified) from the sun's ultraviolet rays, etc. This area affects the transmission and reflection of radio waves. It is divided into three regions: the D region (at 35 to 55 miles [56 to 88 kilometers]), the E Region (Heaviside-Kennelly Layer, 55 to 95 miles [56 to 153 kilometers]), and the F Region (Appleton Layer, 95 to 250 miles [153 to 402 kilometers]).

What are the **Van Allen belts**?

The Van Allen belts (or zones) are two regions of highly charged particles above the Earth's equator trapped by the magnetic field that surrounds the Earth. Also called the magnetosphere, the first belt extends from a few hundred to about 2,000 miles (3,200 kilometers) above the Earth's surface and the second is between 9,000 and 12,000 miles (14,500 to 19,000 kilometers). The particles, mainly protons and electrons, come from the solar wind and cosmic rays. The belts are named in honor of James Van Allen (b. 1914), the American physicist who discovered them in 1958 and 1959, with the aid of radiation counters carried aboard the artificial satellites, *Explorer I* (1958) and *Pioneer 3* (1959).

Why is the **sky blue**?

The sunlight interacting with the Earth's atmosphere makes the sky blue. In outer space the astronauts see blackness because outer space has no atmosphere. Sunlight consists of light waves of varying wavelengths, each of which is seen as a different color. The minute particles of matter and molecules of air in the atmosphere intercept and scatter the white light of the sun. A larger portion of the blue color in white light is scattered, more so than any other color because the blue wavelengths are the shortest. When the size of atmospheric particles are smaller than the wavelengths of the colors, selective scattering occurs—the particles only scatter one color and the atmosphere will appear to be that color. Blue wavelengths especially are affected, bouncing off the air particles to become visible. This is why the sun looks yellow (yellow equals white minus blue). At sunset, the sky changes color because as the sun drops to the horizon, sunlight has more atmosphere to pass through and loses more of its blue wavelengths (the shortest of all the colors). The orange and red, having the longer wavelengths and making up more of sunlight at this distance, are most likely to be scattered by the air particles.

PHYSICAL CHARACTERISTICS, ETC.

See also: Space—Planets and Moons

What is the **mass** of the **Earth**?

The mass of the Earth is estimated to be 6 sextillion, 588 quintillion short tons (6.6 sextillion short tons) or 5.97×10^{24} kilograms, with the Earth's mean density being 5.515 times that of water (the standard). This is calculated from using the parameters of an ellipsoid adopted by the International Astronomical Union in 1964 and recognized by the International Union of Geodesty and Geophysics in 1967.

What is the **interior of the Earth** like?

The Earth is divided into a number of layers. The topmost layer is the crust, which contains about 0.6% of the Earth's volume. The depth of the crust varies from 3.5 to five miles (five to nine kilometers) beneath the oceans to 50 miles (80 kilometers) beneath some mountain ranges. The crust is formed primarily of rocks such as granite and basalt.

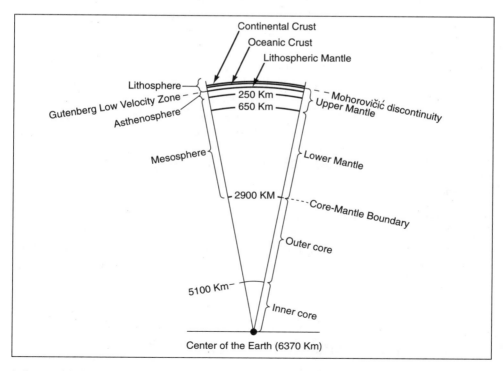

A diagram of the interior of the Earth.

What causes sinkholes?

A sinkhole is a depression shaped like a well or funnel that occurs in a land surface. Most common in limestone regions, sinkholes are usually formed by the dissolving action of groundwater or the seepage of above-ground streams into the limestone below, causing cracks or fractures in subterranean rock. The collapse of cave roofs can also cause large sinkholes. The resulting depression may be several miles in diameter.

Between the crust and the mantle is a boundary known as the Mohorovičič discontinuity (or Moho for short), named for the Croatian seismologist, Andrija Mohorovičič (1857–1936), who discovered it in 1909. Below the Moho is the mantle, extending down about 1,800 miles (2,900 kilometers). The mantle is composed mostly of oxygen, iron, silicon, and magnesium, and accounts for about 82% of the Earth's volume. Although mostly solid, the upper part of the mantle, called the asthenosphere, is partially liquid.

The core-mantle boundary, also called the Gutenberg discontinuity for the German-American seismologist, Beno Gutenberg (1889–1960), separates the mantle from the core. Made up primarily of nickel and iron, the core contains about 17% of the Earth's volume. The outer core is liquid and extends from the base of the mantle to a depth of about 3,200 miles (5,155 kilometers). The solid inner core reaches from the bottom of the outer core to the center of the Earth, about 3,956 miles (6,371 kilometers) deep. The temperature of the inner core is estimated to be about 7,000°F (3,850°C).

How does the **temperature of the Earth** change as one goes deeper underground?

The Earth's temperature increases with depth. Measurements made in deep mines and drill-holes indicate that the rate of temperature increase varies from place to place in the world, ranging from 59° to 167°F (15 to 75°C) per kilometer in depth. Actual temperature measurements cannot be made beyond the deepest drill-holes, which are a little more than 6.2 miles (10 kilometers) deep. Estimates suggest that the temperatures at the Earth's center can reach values of 5,000°F (2,760°C) or higher.

Which elements are contained in the **Earth's crust**?

The most abundant elements in the Earth's crust are listed in the table below. In addition, nickel, copper, lead, zinc, tin, and silver account for less than 0.02% with all other elements comprising 0.48%.

Element	Percentage
Oxygen	47.0
Silicon	28.0
Aluminum	8.0
Iron	4.5
Calcium	3.5
Magnesium	2.5
Sodium	2.5
Potassium	2.5
Titanium	0.4
Hydrogen	0.2
Carbon	0.2
Phosphorous	0.1
Sulfur	0.1

What are the **highest and lowest** points on **Earth**?

The highest point on land is the top of Mt. Everest (in the Himalayas on the Nepal-Tibet border) at 29,028 feet (8,848 meters) above sea level, plus or minus 10 feet (three meters) because of snow. This height was established by the Surveyor General of India in 1954 and accepted by the National Geographic Society. Prior to that the height was taken to be 29,002 feet (8,840 meters). Satellite measurements taken in 1987 indicate that Mt. Everest is 29,864 feet (9,102 meters) high but this measurement has not been adopted by the National Geographic Society.

The lowest point on land is the Dead Sea between Israel and Jordan, which is 1,312 feet (399 meters) below sea level. The lowest point on the Earth's surface is thought to be in the Marianas Trench in the western Pacific Ocean extending from southeast of Guam to northwest of the Marianas Islands. It has been measured as 36,198 feet (11,034 meters) below sea level.

What are the **highest and lowest** elevations in the United States?

Named in honor of U.S. president William McKinley (1843–1901), Mt. McKinley, Alaska, at 20,320 feet (6,194 meters), is the highest point in the United States and North America. Located in central Alaska, it belongs to the Alaska Range. Its south peak measures 20,320 feet (6,194 meters) high and the north peak is 19,470 feet (5,931 meters) high. It boasts one of the world's largest unbroken precipices and is the main scenic attraction at Denali National Park. Denali means the "high one" or the "great one" and is a native American name sometimes used for Mt. McKinley. Mt. Whitney, California, at 14,494 feet (4,421 meters), is the highest point in the continental United States. Death Valley, California, at 282 feet (86 meters) below sea level, is the lowest point in the United States and in the western hemisphere.

How much of the **Earth's surface** is land and how much is water?

Approximately 30% of the Earth's surface is land. This is about 57,259,000 square miles (148,300,000 square kilometers). The area of the Earth's water surface is approximately 139,692,000 square miles (361,800,000 square kilometers), or 70% of the total surface area.

WATER

If the Earth were a uniform sphere, **how much water** would cover the surface?

It is estimated that 97% of all water in the world or over one quadrillion acre-feet ($1,234 \times 10^{15}$ cubic meters) is contained within the oceans. If the Earth were a uniform sphere, this volume of water would cover the Earth to a depth of 800 feet (244 meters).

If you **melted all the ice** in the world, how high would the oceans rise?

If you melted all the ice in the world, some 23 million cubic kilometers in all, the oceans would rise 1.7% or about 180 feet (60 meters), enough for example, for 20 stories of the Empire State Building to be underwater.

What fraction of an **iceberg** shows above water?

Only one seventh to one-tenth of an iceberg's mass shows above water.

What is an **aquifer**?

Some rocks of the upper part of the Earth's crust contain many small holes, or pores. When these holes are large or are joined together so that water can flow through them easily, the rock is considered to be permeable. A large body of permeable rock in which water is stored and flows through is called an aquifer (from the Latin for "water" and "to bear"). Sandstones and gravels are excellent examples of permeable rock.

As water reservoirs, aquifers provide about 60% of American drinking water. The huge Ogallala Aquifer, underlying about two million acres of the Great Plains, is a major source of water for the central United States. It has been estimated that after oceans (containing 850 million cubic miles [1,370 million cubic kilometers] of water), aquifers, with an estimated 31 million cubic miles (50 million cubic kilometers), are the second largest store of water. Water is purified as it is filtered through the rock, but it can be polluted by spills, dumps, acid rain, and other causes. In addition, recharging of water by rainfall often cannot keep up with the volume removed by heavy pumping. The Ogallala Aquifer's supply of water could be depleted by 25% in the year 2020.

What is the **chemical composition** of the **ocean**?

The ocean contains every known naturally occurring element plus various gases, chemical compounds, and minerals. Below is a sampling of the most abundant chemicals.

Constituent	Concentration (parts per million)
Chloride	18,980
Sodium	10,560
Sulfate	2,560
Magnesium	1,272
Calcium	400
Potassium	380
Bicarbonate	142
Bromide	65
Strontium	13
Boron	4.6
Fluoride	1.4

Why is the **sea blue**?

There is no single cause for the colors of the sea. What is seen depends in part on when and from where the sea is observed. Eminent authority can be found to support almost any explanation. Some explanations include absorption and scattering of light by pure water; suspended matter in sea water; the atmosphere; and color and brightness variations of the sky. For example, one theory is that when sunlight hits seawater, part of the white light, composed of different wavelengths of various colors, is absorbed, and some of the wavelengths are scattered after colliding with the water molecules. In clear water, red and infrared light are greatly absorbed but blue is least absorbed, so that the blue wavelengths are reflected out of the water. The blue effect requires a minimum depth of 10 feet (three meters) of water.

How far can **sunlight penetrate** into the ocean?

Because seawater is relatively transparent, approximately 5% of sunlight can penetrate clean ocean water to a depth of 262 feet (80 meters). When the water is turbid (cloudy) due to currents, mixing of silt, increased growth of algae, or other factors, the depth of penetration is reduced to less than 164 feet (50 meters).

How **deep** is the ocean?

The average depth of the ocean floor is 13,124 feet (4,000 meters). The average depth of the four major oceans is given below:

Ocean	Average depth	
	Feet	Meters
Pacific	13,740	4,188
Atlantic	12,254	3,735
Indian	12,740	3,872
Arctic	3,407	1,038
Average overall	13,124	4,000

There are great variations in depth because the ocean floor is often very rugged. The greatest depth variations occur in deep, narrow depressions known as trenches along the margins of the continental plates. The deepest measurements made—36,198 feet (11,034 meters), deeper than the height of the world's tallest mountains—was taken in Mariana Trench east of the Mariana Islands. In January 1960, the French oceanographer Jacques Piccard, together with the United States Navy Lieutenant David Walsh, took the bathyscaphe *Trieste* to the bottom of the Mariana Trench.

Ocean	Deepest point	Depth	
		Feet	Meters
Pacific	Mariana Trench	36,200	11,033
Atlantic	Puerto Rico Trench	28,374	8,648
Indian	Java Trench	25,344	7,725
Arctic	Eurasia Basin	17,881	5,450

What causes **waves** in the ocean?

The most common cause of surface waves is air movement (the wind). Waves within the ocean can be caused by tides, interactions among waves, submarine earthquakes or volcanic activity, and atmospheric disturbances. Wave size depends on wind speed, wind duration, and the distance of water over which the wind blows. The longer the distance the wind travels over water, or the harder it blows, the higher the waves. As the wind blows over water it tries to drag the surface of the water with it. The surface cannot move as fast as air, so it rises. When it rises, gravity pulls the water back, carrying the falling water's momentum below the surface. Water pressure from below pushes this swell back up again. The tug of war between gravity and water pressure constitutes wave motion. Capillary waves are caused by breezes of less than two knots. At 13 knots the waves grow taller and faster than they grow longer, and their steepness cause them to break, forming whitecaps. For a whitecap to form, the wave height must be one-seventh the distance between wave crests.

What is a **tidal bore**?

A tidal bore is a large, turbulent, wall-like wave of water that moves inland or upriver as an incoming tidal current surges against the flow of a more narrow and shallow river, bay, or estuary. It can be 10 to 16 feet (three to five meters) high and move rapidly (10 to 15 knots) upstream with and faster than the rising tide.

Where are the world's **highest tides**?

The Bay of Fundy (New Brunswick, Canada) has the world's highest tides. They average about 45 feet (14 meters) high in the northern part of the bay, far surpassing the world average of 2.5 feet (0.8 meter).

What is the difference between an **ocean** and a **sea**?

There is no neatly defined distinction between ocean and sea. One definition says the ocean is a great body of interconnecting salt water that covers 71% of the Earth's surface. There are four major oceans—the Arctic, Atlantic, Indian, and Pacific—but some sources do not include the Arctic Ocean, calling it a marginal sea. The terms "ocean" and "sea" are often used interchangeably but a sea is generally considered to be smaller than an ocean. The name is often given to saltwater areas on the margins of an ocean, such as the Mediterranean Sea.

How **salty** is seawater?

Sea water is, on average, 3.3 to 3.7% salt. The amount of salt varies from place to place. In areas where large quantities of fresh water are supplied by melting ice, rivers, or rainfall, such as the Arctic or Antarctic, the level of salinity is lower. Areas such as the Persian Gulf and the Red Sea have salt contents over 4.2%. If all the salt in the ocean were dried, it would form a mass of solid salt the size of Africa. Most of the ocean salt comes from processes of dissolving and leaking from the solid Earth over hundreds of millions of years. Some is the result of salty volcanic rock that flows up from a giant rift that runs through all the ocean's basins.

Is the **Dead Sea** really dead?

Because the Dead Sea, on the boundary between Israel and Jordan, is the lowest body of water on the Earth's surface, any water that flows into it has no outflow. It is called "dead" because its extreme salinity makes impossible any animal or vegetable life except bacteria. Fish introduced into the sea by the Jordan River or by smaller streams die instantly. The only plant life consists primarily of halophytes (plants that grow in salty or alkaline soil). The concentration of salt increases toward the bottom of the lake. The water also has a high density so bathers float on the surface easily.

How much salt is in **brackish water**?

Brackish water has a saline (salt) content between that of fresh water and sea water. It is neither fresh nor salty, but somewhere in between. Brackish waters are usually regarded as those containing 0.5 to 30 parts per thousand salt, while the average saltiness of seawater is 35 parts per thousand.

What is the **bearing capacity of ice** on a lake?

The following chart indicates the maximum safe load. It applies only to clear lake ice that has not been heavily traveled. For early winter slush ice, ice thickness should be doubled for safety.

| Ice thickness | | | Maximum safe load | |
Inches	Centimeters	Examples	Tons	Kilograms
2	5	One person on foot		
3	7.6	Group in single file		
7.5	19	Car or snowmobiles	2	907.2
8	20.3	Light truck	2½	1,361
10	25.4	Medium truck	3½	1,814.4
12	30.5	Heavy truck	9	7,257.6
15	38		10	9,072
20	50.8		25	22,680

Where is the world's **deepest lake**?

Lake Baikal, located in southeast Siberia, Russia, is approximately 5,371 feet (1,638 meters) deep at its maximum depth, Olkhon Crevice, making it the deepest lake in the world. Lake Tanganyika in Tanzania and Zaire is the second deepest lake, with a depth of 4,708 feet (1,435 meters).

Where are the **five largest lakes** in the world located?

| Location | Area | | Length | | Depth | |
	Square miles	Square km[a]	Miles	Km[a]	Feet	Meters
Caspian Sea[b], Asia-Europe	143,244	370,922	760	1,225	3,363	1,025
Superior, North America	31,700	82,103	350	560	1,330	406
Victoria, Africa	26,828	69,464	250	360	270	85
Aralb, Asia	24,904	64,501	280	450	220	67
Huron, North America	23,010	59,600	206	330	750	229

[a]-Kilometers − [b]-Salt water lake

Which of the **Great Lakes** is the largest?

| Lake | Surface area | | Maximum depth | |
	Square miles	Square kilometers	Feet	Meters
Superior	31,700	82,103	1,333	406
Huron	23,010	59,600	750	229

| Lake | Surface area | | Maximum depth | |
	Square miles	Square kilometers	Feet	Meters
Michigan	22,300	57,757	923	281
Erie	9,910	25,667	210	64
Ontario	7,540	19,529	802	244

The North American Great Lakes form a single watershed with one common outlet to the sea—the St. Lawrence Seaway. The total volume of all five basins is 6,000 trillion gallons (22.7 trillion liters). Only Lake Michigan lies wholly within the United States borders; the others share their boundaries with Canada. Some believe that Lake Huron and Lake Michigan are two lobes of one lake, since they are the same elevation and are connected by the 120-foot (36.5-meter) deep Strait of Mackinac, which is 3.6 to five miles (six to eight kilometers) wide. Gage records indicate that they both have similar water level regimes and mean long term behavior, so that hydrologically thay act as one lake. Historically they were considered two by the explorers who named them, but this is considered a misnomer by some.

What is an **oxbow lake**?

An oxbow lake is a crescent-shaped lake lying alongside a winding river, formed when a meander (a bend or loop in the river) becomes separated from the main stream. Erosion and deposition tend to accentuate the meander, with the faster-flowing water on the outside edges of the curves eroding the banks, while the slower-moving water on the inside edges deposits silt on the opposite banks. Over time, this process widens the loop of the meander, while narrowing the neck of land dividing the straight path of the river, until the neck vanishes and the river runs past the isolated meander. Without a current to keep it clear, the narrow horseshoe-shaped lake silts up. During the comparatively brief period after the meander is cut off and before it fills with silt, it is an oxbow lake.

A different explanation for the mechanics involved in cutting off a meander has been suggested by laboratory experiments. A stream needs a minimum slope or gradient (horizontal distance divided by height change) to be able to flow and to transport sediment; a meander decreases the gradient of a stream by increasing the distance that it must cover before dropping to a lower height. If a stream's gradient falls below the minimum required, it will tend to cut across the meanders in order to continue flowing.

What is a **yazoo**?

A yazoo is a tributary of a river that runs parallel to the river, being prevented from joining the river because the river has built up high banks. The name is derived from the Yazoo River, a tributary of the Mississippi River, which demonstrates this effect.

What are the **longest rivers** in the world?

The two longest rivers in the world are the Nile in Africa and the Amazon in South America. However, which is the longest is a matter of some debate. The Amazon has several mouths that widen toward the South Atlantic, so the exact point where the river ends is uncertain. If the Pará estuary (the most distant mouth) is counted, its length is approximately 4,195 miles (6,750 kilometers). The length of the Nile as surveyed before the loss of a few miles of meanders due to the formation of Lake Nasser behind the Aswan Dam was 4,145 miles (6,670 kilometers). The table below lists the five longest river systems in the world.

River	Length Miles	Length Kilometers
Nile (Africa)	4,145	6,670
*Amazon (South America)	4,000	6,404
Chang jiang-Yangtze (Asia)	3,964	6,378
Mississippi-Missouri river system (North America)	3,740	6,021
Yenisei-Angara river system (Asia)	3,442	5,540

*excluding Pará estuary

What is the world's **highest waterfall**?

Angel Falls, named after the explorer and bush pilot, Jimmy Angel, on the Carrao tributary in Venezuela is the highest waterfall in the world. It has a total height of 3,212 feet (979 meters) with its longest unbroken drop being 2,648 feet (807 meters).

It is difficult to determine the height of a waterfall because many are composed of several sections rather than one straight drop. The highest waterfall in the United States is Yosemite Falls on a tributary of the Merced River in Yosemite National Park, California, with a total drop of 2,425 feet (739 meters). There are three sections to the Yosemite Falls: Upper Yosemite is 1,430 feet (435 meters); Cascades (middle portion), 675 feet (205 meters); and Lower Yosemite, 320 feet (97 meters).

Why was **Niagara Falls shut down** for thirty hours in 1848?

The volume of Niagara waters depends on the height of Lake Erie at Buffalo, a factor that varies with the direction and intensity of the wind. Changes of as much as eight feet (2.5 meters) in the level of Lake Erie at the Niagara River source have been recorded. On March 29, 1848, a gale drove the floating ice in Lake Erie to the lake outlet, quickly blocking that narrow channel and shutting off a large proportion of the river's flow. Eyewitness accounts stated that the American falls were passable on foot, but for that day only.

When will Niagara Falls disappear?

The water dropping over Niagara Falls digs great plunge pools at the base, undermining the shale cliff and causing the hard limestone cap to cave in. Niagara has eaten itself seven miles (11 kilometers) upstream since it was formed 10,000 years ago. At this rate, it will disappear into Lake Erie in 22,800 years. The Niagara River connects Lake Erie with Lake Ontario, and marks the U.S.–Canada boundary (New York–Ontario).

LAND

See also: Space—Planets and Moons

Are there **tides in the solid part of the Earth** as well as in its waters?

The solid Earth is distorted about 4.5 to 14 inches (11.4 to 35.6 centimeters) by the gravitational pull of the sun and moon. It is the same gravitational pull that creates the tides of the waters. When the moon's gravity pulls water on the side of the Earth near to it, it pulls the solid body of the Earth on the opposite side away from the water to create bulges on both sides, and causing high tides. These occur every 12.5 hours. Low tides occur in those places from which the water is drained to flow into the two high-tide bulges. The sun causes tides on the Earth that are about 33 to 46% as high as those due to the moon. During a new moon or a full moon when the sun and moon are in a straight line, the tides of the moon and the sun reinforce each other to make high tides higher; these are called spring tides. At the quarter moons, the sun and moon are out of step (at right angles), the tides are less extreme than usual; these are called neap tides. Smaller bodies of water, such as lakes, have no tides because the whole body of water is raised all at once, along with the land beneath it.

Do the **continents move**?

In 1912, a German geologist, Alfred Lothar Wegener (1880–1930), theorized that the continents had drifted or floated apart to their present locations and that once all the continents had been a single land mass near Antarctica, which is called *Pangaea* (from the Greek word meaning *all-earth*). Pangaea then broke apart some 200 million years ago into two major continents called Laurasia and Gondwanaland. These two conti-

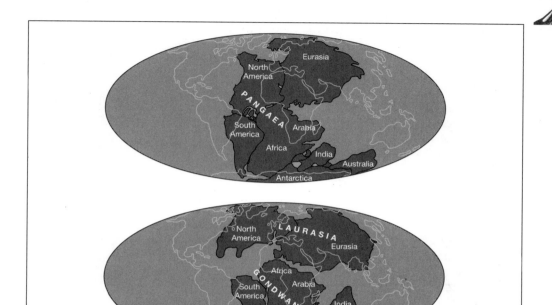

The Pangaea supercontinent (top) and its break up into Laurasia and Gondwanaland.

nents continued drifting and separating until the continents evolved their present shapes and positions. Wegener's theory was discounted but it has since been found that the continents do move sideways (not drift) at an estimated 0.75 inch (19 millimeters) annually because of the action of plate tectonics. American geologist William Maurice Ewing (1906–1974) and Harry Hammond Hess (1906–1969) proposed that the Earth's crust is not a solid mass, but composed of eight major and seven minor plates that can move apart, slide by each other, collide, or override each other. Where these plates meet are major areas of mountain-building, earthquakes, and volcanoes.

How much of the Earth's surface is **covered with ice?**

About 10.4% of the world's land surface is glaciated, or permanently covered with ice. Approximately 6,020,000 square miles (15,600,000 square kilometers) are covered by ice in the form of ice sheets, ice caps, or glaciers. An ice sheet is a body of ice that blankets an area of land, completely covering its mountains and valleys. Ice sheets have an area of over 19,000 square miles (50,000 square kilometers); ice caps are smaller. Glaciers are larger masses of ice that flow, under the force of gravity, at a rate of between 10 and 1,000 feet (three to 300 meters) per year. Glaciers on steep slopes flow faster. For example, the Quarayoq Glacier in Greenland averages 65 to 80 feet (20 to 24 meters) per day. The areas of glaciation in some parts of the world are:

Place	Area	
	Square miles	Square kilometers
Antarctica	5,250,000	12,588,000
North Polar Regions (Greenland, Northern Canada, Arctic Ocean islands)	799,000	2,070,000
Asia	44,000	115,800
Alaska & Rocky Mountains	29,700	76,900
South America	10,200	26,500
Iceland	4,699	12,170
Alpine Europe	3,580	9,280
New Zealand	391	1,015
Africa	5	12

How much of the Earth's surface is **permanently frozen**?

About one-fifth of the Earth's land is permafrost, or ground that is permanently frozen. This classification is based entirely on temperature and disregards the composition of the land. It can include bedrock, sod, ice, sand, gravel, or any other type of material in which the temperature has been below freezing for over two years. Nearly all permafrost is thousands of years old.

Where are the **northernmost** and **southernmost** points of land?

The most northern point of land is Cape Morris K. Jesup on the northeastern extremity of Greenland. It is at 83 degrees, 39 minutes north latitude and is 440 miles (708 kilometers) from the North Pole. However, the *Guinness Book of Records* reports that an islet of 100 feet (30 meters) across, called Oodaq, is more northerly at 83 degrees, 40 minutes north latitude and 438.9 miles (706 kilometers) from the North Pole. The southernmost point of land is the South Pole (since the South Pole, unlike the North Pole, is on land).

In the United States, the northernmost point of land is Point Barrow, Alaska (71 degrees, 23 minutes north latitude), and the southernmost point of land is Ka Lae or South Cape (18 degrees, 55 minutes north latitude) on the island of Hawaii. In the 48 contiguous states, the northernmost point is Northwest Angle, Minnesota (49 degrees, 23 minutes north latitude); the southernmost point is Key West, Florida (24 degrees, 33 minutes north latitude).

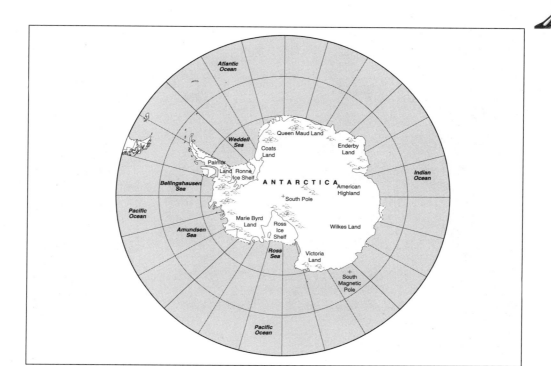

Antarctica.

How thick is the ice that covers **Antarctica**?

The ice that covers Antarctica is 15,700 feet (4,785 meters) in depth at its thickest point. This is about ten times taller than the Sears Tower in Chicago, the world's tallest building. However, the average thickness is 7,100 feet (2,164 meters).

Who was the **first person on Antarctica**?

Historians are unsure who first set foot on Antarctica, the fifth largest continent covering 10 percent of the Earth's surface with its area of 5.4 million square miles (14 million square kilometers). In 1773–1775 British Captain James Cook (1728–1779) circumnavigated the continent. American explorer Nathaniel Palmer (1799–1877) discovered Palmer Peninsula in 1820, without realizing that this was a continent. In this the same year Fabian Gottlieb von Bellingshausen (1779–1852) sighted the Antarctic continent. American sealer John Davis went ashore at Hughes Bay on February 7, 1821. In 1823, sealer James Weddell (1787–1834) traveled the farthest south (74 degrees south) that anyone had until that time and entered what is now called the Weddell Sea. In 1840, American Charles Wilkes (1798–1877), who followed the coast for 1,500 miles, announced the existence of Antarctica as a continent. In 1841, Sir

87

Hoodoos at Bryce Canyon, Utah.

James Clark Ross (1800–1862) discovered Victoria Land, Ross Island, Mount Erebus, and the Ross Ice Shelf. In 1895, the whaler Henryk Bull landed on the Antarctic continent. Norwegian explorer Roald Amundsen (1872–1928) was the first to reach the South Pole on December 14, 1911. Thirty-four days later, Amundsen's rival Robert Falcon Scott (1868–1912) stood at the South Pole, the second to do so, but he and his companions died upon their return trip.

When was the **Ice Age**?

Ice ages, or glacial periods, have occurred at irregular intervals for over 2.3 billion years. During an ice age, sheets of ice cover large portions of the continents. The exact reasons for the changes in the Earth's climate are not known, although some think they are caused by changes in the Earth's orbit around the sun.

The Great Ice Age occurred during the Pleistocene Epoch, which began about two million years ago and lasted until 11,000 years ago. At its height, about 27% of the world's present land area was covered by ice. In North America, the ice covered Canada and moved southward to New Jersey; in the Midwest, it reached as far south as St. Louis. Small glaciers and ice caps also covered the western mountains. Greenland was covered in ice as it is today. In Europe, ice moved down from Scandinavia into

Germany and Poland; the British Isles and the Alps also had ice caps. Glaciers also covered the northern plains of Russia, the plateaus of Central Asia, Siberia, and the Kamchetka Peninsula.

The glaciers' effect on the United States can still be seen. The drainage of the Ohio River and the position of the Great Lakes were influenced by the glaciers. The rich soil of the Midwest is mostly glacial in origin. Rainfall in areas south of the glaciers formed large lakes in Utah, Nevada, and California. The Great Salt Lake in Utah is a remnant of one of these lakes. The large ice sheets locked up a lot of water; sea level fell about 450 feet (137 meters) below what it is today. As a result, some states, such as Florida, were much larger during the ice age.

The glaciers of the last ice age retreated about 11,000 years ago. Some believe that the ice age is not over yet; the glaciers follow a cycle of advance and retreat many times. There are still areas of the Earth covered by ice and this may be a time in between glacial advances.

What is a **moraine**?

A moraine is a mound, ridge, or any other distinct accumulation of unsorted, unstratified material or drift, deposited chiefly by direct action of glacier ice.

What is a **hoodoo**?

A hoodoo is a fanciful name for a grotesque rock pinnacle or pedestal, usually of sandstone, that is the result of weathering in a semi-arid region. An outstanding example of hoodoos occurs in the Wasatch Formation at Bryce Canyon, Utah.

Where are the world's **largest deserts**?

A desert is an area that receives little precipitation and has little plant cover. Many deserts form a band north and south of the equator at about 20 degrees latitude because moisture-bearing winds do not release their rain over these areas. As the moisture-bearing winds from the higher latitudes approach the equator, their temperatures increase and they rise higher and higher in the atmosphere. When the winds arrive over the equatorial areas and come in contact with the colder parts of the Earth's atmosphere, they cool down and release all their water to create the tropical rain forests near the equator.

The Sahara desert is three times the size of the Mediterranean Sea. In the United States, the largest desert is the Mojave Desert in southern California with an area of 15,000 square miles (38,900 square kilometers).

Desert	Location	Area	
		Square miles	Square kilometers
Sahara	North Africa	3,500,000	9,065,000
Gobi	Mongolia-China	500,000	1,295,000
Kalahari	Southern Africa	225,000	582,800
Great Sandy	Australia	150,000	338,500
Great Victoria	Australia	150,000	338,500

Are all craters part of a volcano?

No, not all craters are of volcanic origin. A crater is a nearly circular area of deformed sedimentary rocks, with a central vent-like depression. Some craters are caused by the collapse of the surface when underground salt or limestone dissolves. The withdrawal of groundwater and the melting of glacial ice can also cause the surface to collapse, forming a crater.

Craters are also caused by large meteorites, comets, and asteroids that hit the Earth. A notable impact crater is Meteor Crater near Winslow, Arizona. It is 4,000 feet (1,219 meters) in diameter, 600 feet (183 meters) deep and is estimated to have been formed 30,000 to 50,000 years ago.

How is speleothem defined?

Speleothem is a term given to those cave features that form after a cave itself has formed. They are secondary mineral deposits that are created by the solidification of fluids or from chemical solutions. These mineral deposits usually contain calcium carbonate ($CaCO_3$) or limestone, but gypsum or silica may also be found. Stalactites, stalagmites, soda straws, cave coral, boxwork and cave pearls are all types of speleothems.

What is a tufa?

It is a general name for calcium carbonate ($CaCO_3$) deposits or spongy porous limestone found at springs in limestone areas, or in caves as massive stalactite or stalagmite deposits. *Tufa*, derived from the Italian word for "soft rock," is formed by the precipitation of calcite from the water of streams and springs.

What is the difference between spelunking and speleology?

Spelunking, or sport caving, is exploring caves as a hobby or for recreation. Speleology is the scientific study of caves and related phenomena, such as the world's deepest

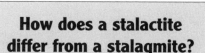

How does a stalactite differ from a stalagmite?

A stalactite is a conical or cylindrical calcite ($CaCO_3$) formation hanging from a cave roof. It forms from the centuries-long buildup of mineral deposits resulting from the seepage of water from the limestone rock above the cave. This water containing calcium bicarbonate evaporates, losing some carbon dioxide, to deposit small quantities of calcium carbonate (carbonate of lime), which eventually forms a stalactite.

A stalagmite is a stone formation that develops upward from the cave floor and resembles an icicle upside down. Formed from water containing calcite that drips from the limestone walls and roof of the cave, it sometimes joins a stalactite to form a column.

cave, Réseau Jean Bernard, Haute Savoie, France with a depth of 5,256 feet (1,602 meters), or the world's longest cave system, Mammoth Cave in Kentucky, with a length of 348 miles (560 kilometers).

What and where is the **continental divide** of North America?

The Continental Divide, also known as the Great Divide, is a continuous ridge of peaks in the Rocky Mountains that marks the watershed separating easterly flowing waters from westerly flowing waters in North America. To the east of the Continental Divide, water drains into Hudson Bay or the Mississippi River before reaching the Atlantic Ocean. To the west, water generally flows through the Columbia River or the Colorado River on its way to the Pacific Ocean.

Which **natural attractions** in the United States are the most popular?

1. The Grand Canyon, Arizona
2. Yellowstone National Park, Wyoming
3. Niagara Falls, New York
4. Mount McKinley, Alaska
5. California's "Big Trees": the sequoias and redwoods
6. Hawaii's volcanoes
7. Florida's Everglades

How long is the Grand Canyon?

The Grand Canyon, cut out by the Colorado River over a period of 15 million years in the northwest corner of Arizona, is the largest land gorge in the world. It is four to 13 miles (6.4 to 21 kilometers) wide at its brim, 4,000 to 5,500 feet (1,219 to 1,676 meters) deep, and 217 miles (349 kilometers) long, extending from the mouth of the Little Colorado River to Grand Wash Cliffs (and 277 miles, 600 feet [445.88 kilometers] if Marble Canyon is included).

The Grand Canyon

However, it is not the deepest canyon in the United States; that distinction belongs to Kings Canyon, which runs through the Sierra and Sequoia National Forests near East Fresno, California, with its deepest point being 8,200 feet (2,500 meters). Hell's Canyon of the Snake River between Idaho and Oregon is the deepest United States canyon in low-relief territory. Also called the Grand Canyon of the Snake, it plunges 7,900 feet (2,408 meters) down from Devil Mountain to the Snake River.

What are the LaBrea tar pits?

The tar pits are located in an area of Los Angeles, California, formerly known as Rancho LaBrea. Heavy, sticky tar oozed out of the Earth, the scum from great petroleum reservoirs far underground. The pools were cruel traps for uncounted numbers of animals. Today the tar pits are a part of Hancock Park where many fossil remains are displayed along with life-sized reconstructions of these prehistoric species.

The tar pits were first recognized as a fossil site in 1875. However, scientists did not systematically excavate the area until 1901. By comparing Rancho La Brea's fossil specimens with their nearest living relatives, paleontologists have a greater understanding of the climate, vegetation and animal life in the area during the Ice Age. Perhaps the most impressive fossil bones recovered belong to such large extinct mammals as the imperial mammoth and the saber-toothed cat. Paleontologists have even found the remains of the western horse and the camel, which originated in North America, migrated to other parts of the world, and became extinct in North America at the end of the Ice Age.

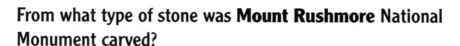

From what type of stone was **Mount Rushmore** National Monument carved?

Granite. The monument, in the Black Hills of southwestern South Dakota, depicts the 60-foot high (18-meter high) faces of four United States presidents: George Washington, Thomas Jefferson, Abraham Lincoln, and Theodore Roosevelt. Sculptor Gutzon Borglum (1867–1941) designed the monument, but died before the completion of the project; his son, Lincoln, finished it. From 1927 to 1941, 360 people, mostly construction workers, drillers, and miners, "carved" the figures using dynamite.

What is the composition of the **Rock of Gibraltar**?

It is composed of gray limestone, with a dark shale overlay on parts of its western slopes. Located on a peninsula at the southern extremity of Spain, the Rock of Gibraltar is a mountain at the east end of the Strait of Gibraltar, the narrow passage between the Atlantic Ocean and the Mediterranean Sea. "The Rock" is 1,398 feet (425 meters) tall at its highest point.

VOLCANOES AND EARTHQUAKES

How many **kinds of volcanoes** are there?

Volcanoes are usually cone-shaped hills or mountains built around a vent connecting to reservoirs of molten rock, or magma, below the surface of the Earth. At times the molten rock is forced upwards by gas pressure until it breaks through weak spots in the Earth's crust. The magma erupts forth as lava flows or shoots into the air as clouds of lava fragments, ash, and dust. The accumulation of debris from eruptions cause the volcano to grow in size. There are four kinds of volcanoes:

Cinder cones are built of lava fragments. They have slopes of 30 degrees to 40 degrees and seldom exceed 1,640 feet (500 meters) in height. Sunset Crater in Arizona and Paricutin in Mexico are examples of cinder cones.

Composite cones are made of alternating layers of lava and ash. They are characterized by slopes of up to 30 degrees at the summit, tapering off to five degrees at the base. Mount Fuji in Japan and Mount St. Helens in Washington are composite cone volcanoes.

Shield volcanoes are built primarily of lava flows. Their slopes are seldom more than 10 degrees at the summit and two degrees at the base. The Hawaiian Islands are clusters of shield volcanoes. Mauna Loa is the world's largest active volcano, rising 13,653 feet (4,161 meters) above sea level.

93

Lava domes are made of viscous, pasty lava squeezed like toothpaste from a tube. Examples of lava domes are Lassen Peak and Mono Dome in California.

Where is the **Circle of Fire**?

The belt of volcanoes bordering the Pacific Ocean is often called the "Circle of Fire" or the "Ring of Fire." The Earth's crust is composed of 15 pieces, called plates, which "float" on the partially molten layer below them. Most volcanoes, earthquakes, and mountain building occur along the unstable plate boundaries. The Circle of Fire marks the boundary between the plate underlying the Pacific Ocean and the surrounding plates. It runs up the west coast of the Americas from Chile to Alaska (through the Andes Mountains, Central America, Mexico, California, the Cascade Mountains, and the Aleutian Islands) then down the east coast of Asia from Siberia to New Zealand (through Kamchatka, the Kurile Islands, Japan, the Philippines, Celebes, New Guinea, the Solomon Islands, New Caledonia, and New Zealand). Of the 850 active volcanoes in the world, over 75% of them are part of the Circle of Fire.

Which **volcanoes** have been the **most destructive**?

The five most destructive eruptions from volcanoes since 1700 are as follows:

Volcano	Date of eruption	Number killed	Lethal agent
Mt. Tambora, Indonesia	April 5, 1815	92,000	2,000 directly by the volcano, 80,000 from starvation afterwards
Karkatoa, Indonesia	Aug. 26, 1883	36,417	90% killed by a tsunami
Mt. Pelee, Martinque	Aug. 30, 1902	29,025	Pyroclastic flows
Nevada del Ruiz, Colombia	Nov. 13, 1985	23,000	Mud flow
Unzen, Japan	1792	14,300	70% killed by cone collapse; 30% by a tsunami

When did **Mount St. Helens** erupt?

Mount St. Helens, located in southwestern Washington state in the Cascades mountain range, erupted on May 18, 1980. Sixty-one people died as a result of the eruption. This was the first known eruption in the 48 contiguous United States to claim a human life. Geologists call Mount St. Helens a composite volcano (a steep-sided, often symmetrical cone constructed of alternating layers of lava flows, ash, and other volcanic debris). Composite volcanoes tend to erupt explosively. Mount St. Helens and the other active volcanoes in the Cascade Mountains are a part of the "Ring of Fire"— the Pacific zone having frequent and destructive volcanic activity.

Who invented the ancient Chinese earthquake detector?

The detector, invented by Zhang Heng (78–139 A.D.) around 132 A.D., was a copper-domed urn with dragons' heads circling the outside, each containing a bronze ball. Inside the dome was suspended a pendulum that would swing when the ground shook, and knock a ball from the mouth of a dragon into the waiting open mouth of a bronze toad below. The ball made a loud noise and signaled the occurrence of an earthquake. Knowing which ball had been released, one could determine the direction of the earthquake's epicenter (the point on the Earth's surface directly above the quake's point of origin).

Volcanoes have not only been active in Washington, but also in three other U.S. states: California, Alaska, and Hawaii. Lassen Peak is one of several volcanoes in the Cascade Range. It last erupted in 1921. Mount Katmai in Alaska had an eruption in 1912 in which the flood of hot ash formed the Valley of Ten Thousand Smokes 15 miles (24 kilometers) away. And Hawaii has its famed Mauna Loa, which is the world's largest volcano, being 60 miles (97 kilometers) in width at its base.

What is a **tsunami**?

A tsunami is a giant wave set in motion by a large earthquake occurring under or near the ocean that causes the ocean floor to shift vertically. This vertical shift pushes the water ahead of it, starting a tsunami. These are very long waves (100 to 200 miles [161 to 322 kilometers]) with high speeds (500 mph [805 kph]) that, when approaching shallow water, can grow into a 100-foot (30.5-meter) high wave as its wavelength is reduced abruptly. Ocean earthquakes below a magnitude of 6.5 on the Richter scale, and those that shift the sea floor only horizontally, do not produce these destructive waves.

How does a **seismograph** work?

A seismograph records earthquake waves. When an earthquake occurs, three types of waves are generated. The first two, the P and S waves, are propagated within the Earth, while the third, consisting of Love and Rayleigh waves, is propagated along the planet's surface. The P wave travels about 3.5 miles (5.6 kilometers) per second and is is the first wave to reach the surface. The S wave travels at a velocity of a little more than half of the P waves. If the velocities of the different modes of wave propagation are known, **95** the distance between the earthquake and an observation station may be deduced by measuring the time interval between the arrival of the faster and slower waves.

When the ground shakes, the suspended weight of the seismograph, because of its inertia, scarcely moves, but the shaking motion is transmitted to the marker, which leaves a record on the drum.

What is the **Richter scale**?

On a machine called a seismograph, the Richter scale measures the magnitude of an earthquake, i.e., the size of the ground waves generated at the earthquake's source. The scale was devised by American geologist Charles W. Richter (1900–1985) in 1935. Every increase of one number means a tenfold increase in magnitude.

Richter Scale

Magnitude	Possible effects
1	Detectable only by instruments
2	Barely detectable, even near the epicenter
3	Felt indoors
4	Felt by most people; slight damage
5	Felt by all; damage minor to to moderate
6	Moderately destructive
7	Major damage
8	Total and major damage

What is the **modified Mercalli Scale**?

The modified Mercalli Scale is a means of measuring the intesity of an earthquake. Unlike the Richter Scale, which uses mathematical calculation to measure seismic waves, the modified Mercalli Scale uses the effects of an earthquake on the people and structures in a given area to determine its intensity. It was invented by Guiseppe Mercalli (1850–1914) in 1902 and modified by Harry Wood and Frank Neumann in the 1930s to take into consideration such modern inventions as the automobile and the skyscraper.

The Modified Mercalli Scale

I   Only felt by a few under especially favorable circumstances.

II   Felt only by a few sleeping persons, particularly on upper floors of buildings. Some suspended objects may swing.

III Felt quite noticeably indoors, especially on upper floors of buildings, but may not be recognized as an earthquake. Standing automobiles may rock slightly. Vibration like passing of truck.

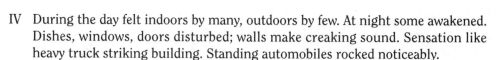
IV   During the day felt indoors by many, outdoors by few. At night some awakened. Dishes, windows, doors disturbed; walls make creaking sound. Sensation like heavy truck striking building. Standing automobiles rocked noticeably.

V   Felt by nearly everyone, many awakened. Some dishes, windows, and so on broken; cracked plaster in a few places; unstable objects overturned. Disturbances of trees, poles, and other tall objects sometimes noticed. Pendulum clocks may stop.

VI   Felt by all; many frightened and run outdoors. Some heavy furniture moved; a few instances of fallen plaster and damaged chimneys. Damage slight.

VII Everybody runs outdoors. Damage negligible in buildings of good design and construction; slight to moderate in well-built ordinary structures; considerable in poorly built or badly designed structures; some chimneys broken. Noticed by persons driving cars.

VIII Damage slight in specially designed structures; considerable in ordinary substantial buildings with partial collapse; great in poorly built structures. Panel walls thrown out of frame structures. Fall of chimneys, factory stacks, columns, monuments, walls. Heavy furniture overturned. Sand and mud ejected in small amounts. Changes in well water. Persons driving cars disturbed.

IX   Damage considerable in specially designed structures; well-designed frame structures thrown out of plumb; great in substantial buildings, with partial collapse. Building shifted off foundations. Ground cracked conspicuously. Underground pipes broken.

X   Some well-built wooden structures destroyed; most masonry and frame structures destroyed with foundations; ground badly cracked. Rails bent. Landslides considerable from river banks and steel slopes. Shifted sand and mud. Water splashed, slopped over banks.

XI   Few, if any, (masonry) structures remain standing. Bridges destroyed. Broad fissures in ground. Underground pipelines completely out of service. Earth slumps and landslips in soft ground. Rails bent greatly.

XII Damage total. Waves seen on ground surface. Lines of sight and level distorted. Objects thrown into the air.

When did the **most severe earthquake** in American history occur?

The New Madrid earthquakes (a series of quakes starting on December 16, 1811, and lasting until March 1812) is considered to be the most severe earthquake event in United States history. It shook more than two-thirds of the United States and was felt in Canada. It changed the level of land by as much as 20 feet (six meters), altered the course of the Mississippi River, and created new lakes, such as Lake St. Francis west of the Mississippi and Reelfoot Lake in Tennessee. Because the area was so sparsely populated, no known loss of life occurred. Scientists agree that at least three, and possibly five, of the quakes had surface wave magnitudes of 8.0 or greater. The largest was probably a magnitude of 8.8, which is larger than any quake yet experienced in California.

Of what magnitude was the **earthquake** that hit **San Francisco** on April 18, 1906?

The historic 1906 San Francisco earthquake took a mighty toll on the city and surrounding area. Over 700 people were killed; the newly constructed $6 million city hall was ruined; the Sonoma Wine Company collapsed, destroying 15 million gallons (57 million liters) of wine. The quake registered 8.3 on the Richter scale and lasted 75 seconds total. Many poorly constructed buildings built on landfills were flattened and the quake destroyed almost all of the gas and water mains. Fires broke out shortly after the quake, and when they were finally eliminated, 3,000 acres of the city, the equivalent of 520 blocks, were charred. Damage was estimated to be $500 million, and many insurance agencies went bankrupt after paying out the claims.

Again on October 17, 1989, an earthquake hit San Francisco, measuring 7.1 on the Richter scale, killing 67 people, and causing billions of dollars worth of damage.

OBSERVATION AND MEASUREMENT

What are the major eras, periods, and epochs in geologic time?

Modern dating techniques have given a range of dates as to when the various geologic time periods have started, as they are listed below:

Era	Period	Epoch	Beginning date (Est. millions of years)
Cenozoic	Quaternary	Holocene	10,000 years ago
		Pleistocene	1.9
	Tertiary	Pliocene	6
		Miocene	25
		Oligocene	38
		Eocene	55
		Paleocene	65

Era	Period	Epoch	Beginning date (Est. millions of years)
Mesozoic	Cretaceous		135
	Jurassic		200
	Triassic		250
Paleozoic	Permian		285
	Carboniferous (divided into Mississippian and Pennsylvanian periods by some in the U.S.)		350
	Devonian		410
	Silurian		425
	Ordovician		500
	Cambrian		570
Precambrian	Proterozoic		2500
	Archeozoic		3800
	Azoic		4600

What is **magnetic declination**?

It is the angle between magnetic north and true north at a given point on the Earth's surface. It varies at different points on the Earth's surface and at different times of the year.

Which direction does a **compass needle** point at the **north pole**?

At the north magnetic pole, the compass needle would be attracted by the ground and point straight down.

What is a **Foucault pendulum**?

An instrument devised by Jean Foucault (1819–1868) in 1851 to prove that the Earth rotates on an axis, the pendulum consisted of a heavy ball suspended by a very long fine wire. Sand beneath the pendulum recorded the plane of rotation of the pendulum over time.

A reconstruction of Foucault's experiment is located in Portland, Oregon at its Convention Center. It swings from a cable 90 feet (27.4 meters) long, making it the longest pendulum in the world.

What is the **prime meridian?**

The north-south lines on a map run from the North Pole to the South Pole and are called "meridians," a word that meant "noon," for when it is noon on one place on the line, it is noon at any other point as well. The lines are used to measure longitudes, or how far east or west a particular place might be, and they are 69 miles (111 kilometers) apart at the equator. The east-west lines are called parallels, and unlike meridians, are all parallel to each other. They measure latitude, or how far north or south a particular place might be. There are 180 lines circling the Earth, one for each degree of latitude. The degrees of both latitude and longitude are divided into 60 minutes, further divided into 60 seconds each.

The prime meridian is the meridian of 0 degrees longitude, used as the origin for measurement of longitude. The meridian of Greenwich, England, is used almost universally for this purpose.

What is **Mercator's projection** for maps?

The Mercator projection is a modification of a standard cylindrical projection, a technique used by cartographers to transfer the spherical proportions of the Earth to the flat surface of a map. For correct proportions, the parallels, or lines of latitude, are spaced at increasing distances toward the poles, resulting in severe exaggeration of size in the polar regions. Greenland, for example, appears five times larger than it actually is. Created by Flemish cartographer Gerardus Mercator in 1569, this projection is useful primarily because compass directions appear as straight lines, making it ideal for navigation.

Who is regarded as the founder of American **geology?**

Born in Scotland, the American William Maclure (1763–1840) was a member of a commission set up to settle claims between the United States and France from 1803 through 1807. In 1809 he made a geographical chart of the United States in which the land areas were divided by rock types. In 1817 he revised and enlarged this map. Maclure wrote the first English language articles and books on United States geology.

When were **relief maps** first used?

The Chinese were the first to use relief maps, in which the contours of the terrain were represented in models. Relief maps in China go back at least to the third century B.C.E. Some early maps were modeled in rice or carved in wood. It is likely that the idea of making relief maps was transmitted from the Chinese to the Arabs and then to Europe. The earliest known relief map in Europe was a map showing part of Austria, made in 1510 by Paul Dox.

What is the Piri Re'is map?

In 1929, a map was found in Constantinople that caused great excitement. Painted on parchment and dated in the Moslem year 919 (1541 according to the Christian calendar), it was signed by an admiral of the Turkish navy known as Piri Re'is. This map appears to be one of the earliest maps of America, and it shows South America and Africa in their correct relative longitudes. The mapmaker also indicated that he had used a map drawn by Columbus for the western part. It was an exciting statement because for several centuries geographers had been trying to find a "lost map of Columbus" supposedly drawn by him in the West Indies.

Who was the first person to map the **Gulf Stream**?

In his travels to and from France as a diplomat, Benjamin Franklin (1706–1790) noticed a difference in speed in the two directions of travel between France and America. He was the first to study ships' reports seriously to determine the cause of the speed variation. As a result, he found that there was a current of warm water coming from the Gulf of Mexico that crossed the North Atlantic Ocean in the direction of Europe. In 1770, Franklin mapped it.

Franklin thought the current started in the Gulf of Mexico. However, the Gulf Stream actually originates in the western Caribbean Sea and moves through the Gulf of Mexico, the Straits of Florida, then north along the east coast of the United States to Cape Hatteras in North Carolina where it becomes northeast. The Gulf Stream eventually breaks up near Newfoundland, Canada, to form smaller currents, or eddies. Some of these eddies blow toward the British Isles and Norway, causing the climate of these regions to be more mild than other areas of northwestern Europe.

What are **Landsat maps**?

They are images of the Earth taken at an altitude of 567 miles (912 kilometers) by an orbiting Landsat satellite, or ERTS (Earth Resources Technology Satellite). The Landsats were originally launched in the 1970s. Rather than cameras, the Landsats use multispectral scanners, which detect visible green and blue wavelengths, and four infrared and near-infrared wavelengths. These scanners can detect differences between soil, rock, water, and vegetation; types of vegetation; states of vegetation (e.g., healthy/unhealthy or underwatered/well-watered); and mineral content. The differences are especially accurate when multiple wavelengths are compared using multi-

101

spectral scanners. Even visible light images have proved useful—some of the earliest Landsat images showed that some small Pacific islands were up to 10 miles (16 kilometers) away from their charted positions.

The results are displayed in "false-color" maps, where the scanner data is represented in shades of easily distinguishable colors—usually, infrared is shown as red, red as green, and green as blue. The maps are used by farmers, oil companies, geologists, foresters, foreign governments, and others interested in land management. Each image covers an area approximately 115 square miles (185 square kilometers). Maps are offered for sale by the United States Geological Survey.

Other systems that produce similar images include the French SPOT satellites, the Russian Salyut and Mir manned space stations, and NASA's Airborne Imaging Spectrometer, which senses 128 infrared bands. NASA's Jet Propulsion Laboratories are developing instruments that will sense 224 bands in infrared, which will be able to detect specific minerals absorbed by plants.

From what distance are **satellite photographs** taken?

U.S. Department of Defense satellites orbit at various distances above the Earth. Some satellites are in low orbit, 100 to 300 miles (160 to 483 kilometers) above the surface, while others are positioned at intermediate altitudes from 500 to 1,000 miles (804 to 1,609 kilometers) high. Some have an altitude of 22,300 miles (35,880 kilometers).

ENVIRONMENT

ECOLOGY, RESOURCES, ETC.

What is a **biome**?

It is a plant and animal community that covers a large geographical area. Complex interactions of climate, geology, soil types, water resources, and latitude all determine the kinds of plants and animals that thrive in different places. Fourteen major ecological zones, called "biomes," exist over five major climatic regions and eight zoogeographical regions. Important land biomes include tundra, coniferous forests, deciduous forests, grasslands, savannas, deserts, chaparral, and tropical rainforests.

How does the process work in a **food chain**?

A food chain is the transfer of food energy from the source in plants through a series of organisms with repeated eating and being eaten. The number of steps or "links" in a sequence is usually four to five. The first trophic level (group of organisms that get their energy the same way) is plants; the animals that eat plants (called herbivores) form the second trophic level. The third level consists of primary carnivores (animal-eating animals like wolves) who eat herbivores, and the fourth level are animals (like killer whales) that eat primary carnivores. Food chains overlap because many organisms eat more than one type of food, so that these chains can look more like food webs. In 1891 German zoologist Karl Semper introduced the food chain concept.

What is a **food web**?

A food web consists of interconnecting food chains. Many animals feed on different **103**

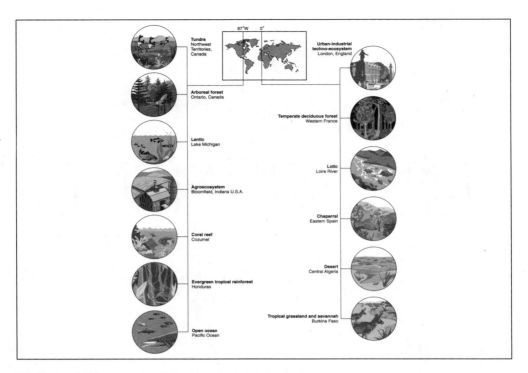

Biomes along 87 degrees west longitude and along 0 degrees longitude.

foods rather than exclusively on one single species of prey or one type of plant. Animals that use a variety of food sources have a greater chance of survival than those with a single food source. Complex food webs provide greater stability to a living community.

What is **eutrophication**?

Eutrophication is a process in which the supply of plant nutrients in a lake or pond is increased. In time, the result of natural eutrophication may be dry land where water once flowed, caused by plant overgrowth.

Natural fertilizers, washed from the soil, result in an accelerated growth of plants, producing overcrowding. As the plants die off, the dead and decaying vegetation depletes the lake's oxygen supply, causing fish to die. The accumulated dead plant and animal material eventually changes a deep lake to a shallow one, then to a swamp, and finally it becomes dry land.

While the process of eutrophication is a natural one, it has been accelerated enormously by human activities. Fertilizers from farms, sewage, industrial wastes, and some detergents all contribute to the problem.

The structure of a eutrophic lake.

How does **ozone** benefit life on Earth?

Ozone in the upper atmosphere (stratosphere) is a major factor in making life on Earth possible. The ozone belt shields the Earth from excessive ultraviolet radiation generated by the sun. Scientists predict that depletion of this layer could lead to increased health problems for humans and disruption of sensitive terrestrial and aquatic ecosystems. Ozone, a form of oxygen with three atoms instead of the normal two, is highly toxic; less than one part per million of this blue-tinged gas is poisonous to humans. While beneficial in the stratosphere, near ground level it is a pollutant that helps form photochemical smog and acid rain.

What is the **greenhouse effect**?

The greenhouse effect is a warming near the Earth's surface that results when the Earth's atmosphere traps the sun's heat. The atmosphere acts much like the glass walls and roof of a greenhouse. The effect was described by John Tyndall (1820–1893) in 1861. It was given the greenhouse analogy much later in 1896 by the Swedish chemist Svante Arrhenius (1859–1927). The greenhouse effect is what makes the **105**

An atmosphere with natural levels of greenhouse gases (left) compared with an atmosphere of increased greenhouse effect (right).

Earth habitable. Without the presence of water vapor, carbon dioxide, and other gases in the atmosphere, too much heat would escape and the Earth would be too cold to sustain life. Carbon dioxide, methane, nitrous oxide, and other "greenhouse gases" absorb the infrared radiation rising from the Earth and holds this heat in the atmosphere instead of reflecting it back into space.

In the 20th century, the increased build-up of carbon dioxide, caused by the burning of fossil fuels, has been a matter of concern. There is some controversy concerning whether the increase noted in the Earth's average temperature is due to the increased amount of carbon dioxide and other gases, or is due to other causes. Volcanic activity, destruction of the rainforests, use of aerosols, and increased agricultural activity may also be contributing factors.

Why is **El Niño** harmful?

Along the west coast of South America, near the end of each calendar year, a warm current of nutrient-poor tropical water moves southward, replacing the cold, nutrient-rich surface water. Because this condition frequently occurs around Christmas,

What is red tide and what causes it?

Red tide is a term used for a brownish or reddish discoloration occurring in ocean, river, or lake water. It is caused by the rapid reproduction of a variety of toxic organisms, especially the toxic red dinoflagellates that are members of the genera *Gymnodidium* and *Gonyaulax*. Some red tides are harmless, but millions of fish may be killed during a "bloom," as the build-up is called. Other red tides can poison shellfish and the birds or humans who eat the contaminated food. Scientists do not fully understand why the "bloom" occurs.

local residents call it *El Niño* (Spanish for child), referring to the Christ child. In most years the warming lasts for only a few weeks. However, when El Niño conditions last for many months, the economic results can be catastrophic. It is this extended episode of extremely warm water that scientists now refer to as El Niño. During a severe El Niño, large numbers of fish and marine plants may die. Decomposition of the dead material depletes the water's oxygen supply, which leads to the bacterial production of huge amounts of smelly hydrogen sulfide. A greatly reduced fish (especially anchovy) harvest affects the world's fishmeal supply, leading to higher prices for poultry and other animals that normally are fed fishmeal.

Studies reveal that El Niño is not an isolated occurrence, but is instead part of a pattern of change in the global circulation of the oceans and atmosphere. The 1982–1983 El Niño was one of the most severe climate events of the twentieth century in both its geographical extent as well as in the degree of warming (14°F or 8°C). The 1986–1987 El Niño might have been responsible in part for record global warmth in 1987—the warmest year in the last 100 years.

How many **acres of tropical forest** does the world lose annually?

Using data from satellite observations, it is estimated that 16.4 to 20.4 million hectares are being destroyed each year (a hectare equals 107,639 square feet [10,000 square meters]). Only 50% of the mature tropical forests remain, with 750 to 800 million hectares of the original 1.5 to 1.6 billion hectares destroyed. Of the two types of tropical forests, wet and dry, the wet or "rain" forests have been incurring the most losses. Latin America has lost 37% of them; Asia, 42%; and Africa, 52%. Logging, fuelwood gathering, and conversion of forests to agriculture are the main causes. Yet tropical forests have been called "green deserts," because their soils are poor in nutrients. The forest vegetation, seemingly lush, has survived through ingenious life-support systems. When the trees are stripped away, the exposed soil deteriorates rapidly, **107** eroded by torrential rains. After the rain ceases, the sun bakes the earth into a hard mass, rendering the soil incapable of vegetative growth.

How rapidly is **deforestation** occurring?

In the 1990 figures given below, the annual deforestation rate is given in percent of forests eradication as well as amount in square kilometers.

Country	Deforestation (square kilometers)	Percent
Brazil	13,820	0.4
Colombia	6,000	1.3
Mexico	7,000	1.5
Indonesia	10,000	0.9
Peru	2,700	0.4
Malaysia	3,100	1.5
Ecuador	3,400	2.4
India	10,000	2.7
Zaire	4,000	0.4
Madagascar	1,500	1.5

How long will it be before all **tropical forests** have been destroyed, if present **rates of destruction** continue?

If present deforestation rates continue, all tropical forests will be cleared in 177 years. These forests contain 155,000 of the 250,000 known plant species and innumerable insect and animal species. Half of all medicines prescribed worldwide are originally derived from wild products, and the United States National Cancer Institute has identified more than two thousand tropical rainforest plants with the potential to fight cancer. Rubber, timber, gums, resins and waxes, pesticides, lubricants, nuts and fruits, flavorings and dyestuffs, steroids, latexes, essential and edible oils, and bamboo are among the forest's products that would be drastically affected by the depletion of the tropical forests.

When did the symbol of **Smokey the Bear** begin to be used for forest fire prevention?

The origin of Smokey Bear can be traced to World War II when the U.S. Forest Service, concerned about maintaining a steady lumber supply for the war effort, wished to educate the public about the dangers of forest fires. They sought volunteer advertising support from the War Advertising Council, and on August 9, 1944, Albert Staehle, a noted illustrator of animals, created Smokey Bear. In 1947, a Los Angeles advertising

A forest (1) destroyed by wildfire (2) and its recovery (3,4).

agency coined the slogan "Only you can prevent forest fires." The campaign gained a living mascot in 1950 when a firefighting crew rescued a male bear cub from a forest fire in the Capital Mountains of New Mexico. Sent to the National Zoo in Washington, D.C. to become Smokey Bear, the animal was a living symbol of forest fire protection until his death in 1976. His remains are buried at the Smokey Bear State Historical Park in Capitan, New Mexico.

What causes the most **forest fires** in the western United States?

Lightning is the single largest cause of forest fires in the western states.

How many acres in the United States are infested by the **gypsy moth**?

In 1990, the total acreage of U.S. land infested by the gypsy moth was reported to be more than seven million acres, four million of which were in Pennsylvania. Since **109**

1869, when Leopold Trouvelot imported gypsy moths from France to Boston in hopes of breeding a better silkworm, these insects have spread across the continent. In one of their record breaking years, 1981, they defoliated almost 13 million acres; in 1993, due to several control measures, the destruction decreased to 1.8 million acres.

Several methods of controlling the insect have been investigated. The *Entomophaga maimaiga* fungus, a natural enemy of the gypsy moth, has been used. A biological insecticide, Gypchek, is registered for use against the gypsy moth and is the only one deemed harmless to other insects. *Bacillus thuringiensis* (Bt), another biological pesticide, and diflubenzuron (Dimilin) are also being studied. However, their undesirable effects on other species are a threat to forest ecosystems. Finding ways of killing gypsy moths without harming the environment still presents a formidable challenge to entomologists.

Who established the first **botanical garden** in the United States?

John Bartram planned and laid out a botanic garden of five to six acres (two to 2.5 hectare) in 1728. It is located in Philadelphia, PA.

How much of the Earth is protected as national parks and similar sites?

Below is a table of protected areas by country for the year 1990.

Country	Percent of total land area
Venezuela	22.2
Bhutan	19.8
Chile	18.2
Botswana	17.4
Panama	16.9
Czechoslovakia	15.4
Namibia	12.7
United States	10.5
Indonesia	9.3
Australia	5.9
Canada	5.0
Mexico	4.8
Brazil	2.4
Madagascar	1.8
Former Soviet Union	1.1
WORLD	4.9

What was the United States' **first national park**?

The U.S. government authorized Yellowstone National Park on March 1, 1872.

What are some of the **largest National Parks**?

The largest National Parks are in Alaska:

Park	Area (acres)
Wrangell-St. Elias	8,331,604
Gates of the Arctic	7,523,888
Denali	4,716,726
Katmai	3,716,000
Glacier Bay	3,225,284
Lake Clark	2,636,839
Kobuk Valley	1,750,421

The five largest parks in the 48 contiguous states are:

Park	Location	Area (acres)
Yellowstone	Idaho, Montana, Wyoming	2,219,791
Everglades	Florida	1,506,599
Grand Canyon	Arizona	1,218,375
Glacier	Montana	1,013,572
Olympic	Washington	922,651

Where is **Hawk Mountain Sanctuary**?

Hawk Mountain Sanctuary, founded in 1934 as the first sanctuary in the world to offer protection to migrating hawks and eagles, is near Harrisburg, Pennsylvania, on the Kittatinny Ridge. Each year between the months of August and December, over 15,000 migrating birds pass by. Rare species such as golden eagles may be seen there.

When was the **first zoo** in the United States established?

The Philadelphia Zoological Garden, chartered in 1859, was the first zoo in the United States. The zoo was delayed by the Civil War, financial difficulties, and restrictions on transporting wild animals. It opened in 1874 on 33 acres, and 282 animals were exhibited.

Who is considered the founder of modern **conservation**?

American naturalist John Muir (1838–1914) was the father of conservation and the founder of the Sierra Club. He fought for the preservation of the Sierra Nevada Mountains in California, and the creation of Yosemite National Park. He directed most of the Sierra Club's conservation efforts and was a lobbyist for the Antiquities Act.

John Muir.

Another prominent influence was George Perkins Marsh (1801–1882), a Vermont lawyer and scholar. His outstanding book *Man and Nature* emphasized the mistakes of past civilizations that resulted in destruction of natural resources. As the conservation movement swept through the country in the last three decades of the 19th century, a number of prominent citizens joined the efforts to conserve natural resources and to preserve wilderness areas. Writer John Burroughs, forester Gifford Pinchot, botanist Charles Sprague Sargent, and editor Robert Underwood Johnson were early advocates of conservation.

Who coined the term **"Spaceship Earth"**?

American inventor and environmentalist Buckminster Fuller (1895–1983) coined the term "Spaceship Earth" as an analogy of the need for technology to be self-contained and to avoid waste.

When was the **Environmental Protection Agency** created?

In 1970, President Richard M. Nixon created the Environmental Protection Agency (EPA) as an independent agency of the U.S. government by executive order. The creation of a federal agency by executive order rather than by an act of the legislative branch is somewhat of an exception to the rule. The EPA was originally designed to consolidate a variety of activities, including environmental research, monitoring, and enforcement activities into one agency.

What is a **"green product"**?

Green products are environmentally safe products that contain no chlorofluorocarbons, are degradable (can decompose), and are made from recycled materials. "Deep-

Who started Earth Day?

The first Earth Day, April 22, 1970, was coordinated by Denis Hayes at the request of Gaylord Nelson, United States Senator from Wisconsin. Nelson is sometimes called the father of Earth Day. His main objective was to organize a nationwide public demonstration so large it would get the attention of politicians and force the environmental issue into the political dialogue of the nation. Important official actions that began soon after the celebration of the first Earth Day were: the establishment of the Environmental Protection Agency (EPA); the creation of the President's Council on Environmental Quality; and the passage of the Clean Air Act, establishing national air quality standards.

green" products are those from small suppliers who build their identities around their claimed environmental virtues. "Greened-up" products come from the industry giants and are environmentally improved versions of established brands.

EXTINCT AND ENDANGERED PLANTS AND ANIMALS

Did **dinosaurs and humans** ever coexist?

No. Dinosaurs first appeared in the Triassic Period (about 220 million years ago) and disappeared at the end of the Cretaceous Period (about 65 million years ago). Modern humans (*Homo sapiens*) appeared only about 25,000 years ago. Movies that show humans and dinosaurs existing together are only Hollywood fantasies.

What were the **smallest** and **largest** dinosaurs?

Compsognathus, a carnivore from the late Jurassic period (131 million years ago), was about the size of a chicken and measured, at most, 35 inches (89 centimeters) from the tip of its snout to the tip of its tail. It probably weighed up to 15 pounds (6.8 kilograms).

The largest species for which a whole skeleton is known is *Brachiosaurus*. A specimen in the Humboldt Museum in Berlin measures 72.75 feet (22.2 meters) long and 46 feet (14 meters) high. It weighed an estimated 34.7 tons (31,480 kilograms). **113**

Brachiosaurus was a four-footed plant-eating dinosaur with a long neck and a long tail and lived from about 155 to 121 million years ago.

How **long** did **dinosaurs live?**

The lifespan has been estimated at 75 to 300 years. Such estimates are educated guesses. From examination of the microstructure of dinosaur bones, scientists have inferred that they matured slowly and probably had proportionately long lifespans.

How does a **mastodon** differ from a **mammoth?**

Although the words are sometimes used interchangeably, the mammoth and the mastodon were two different animals. The mastodon seems to have appeared first and a side branch may have led to the mammoth.

The *mastodon* lived in Africa, Europe, Asia, and North and South America. It appears in the Oligocene (25 to 38 million years ago) and survived until less than one million years ago. It stood a maximum of 10 feet (three meters) tall and was covered with dense woolly hair. Its tusks were straight forward and nearly parallel to each other.

The *mammoth* evolved less than two million years ago and died out about 10 thousand years ago. It lived in North America, Europe, and Asia. Like the mastodon, the mammoth was covered with dense, woolly hair, with a long, coarse layer of outer hair to protect it from the cold. It was somewhat larger than the mastodon, standing 9 to 15 feet (2.7 to 4.5 meters). The mammoth's tusks tended to spiral outward, then up.

The gradual warming of the Earth's climate and the change in environment were probably primary factors in the animals' extinction. But early man killed many of them as well, perhaps hastening the process.

Why did **dinosaurs** become **extinct?**

There are many theories as to why dinosaurs disappeared from the Earth about 65 million years ago. Scientists argue over whether the dinosaurs became extinct gradually or all at once. The gradualists believe that the dinosaur population steadily declined at the end of Cretaceous Period. Numerous reasons have been proposed for this. Some claim the dinosaurs' extinction was caused by biological changes that made them less competitive with other organisms, especially the mammals who were just beginning to appear. Overpopulation has been argued, as has the theory that mammals ate too many dinosaur eggs for the animals to reproduce themselves. Others believe that disease—everything from rickets to constipation—wiped them out.

Changes in climate, continental drift, volcanic eruptions, and shifts in the Earth's axis, orbit, and/or magnetic field have also been held responsible.

The catastrophists argue that a single disasterous event caused the extinction, not only of the dinosaurs, but also of a large number of other species that coexisted with them. In 1980, American physicist Luis Alvarez (1911–1988) and his geologist son, Walter Alvarez (b. 1940), proposed that a large comet or meteoroid struck the Earth 65 million years ago. They pointed out that there is a high concentration of the element iridium in the sediments at the boundary between the Cretaceous and Tertiary Periods. Iridium is rare on Earth, so the only source of such a large amount of it had to be outer space. This iridium anamoly has since been discovered at over 50 sites around the world. In 1990, tiny glass fragments, which could have been caused by the extreme heat of an impact, were identified in Haiti. A 110-mile (177-kilometer) wide crater in the Yucatan Peninsula, long covered by sediments, has been dated to 64.98 million years ago, making it a leading candidate for the site of this impact.

A hit by a large extraterrestrial object, perhaps as much as six miles (9.3 kilometers) wide, would have had a catastrophic effect upon the world's climate. Huge amounts of dust and debris would have been thrown into the atmosphere, reducing the amount of sunlight reaching the surface. Heat from the blast may also have caused large forest fires, which would have added smoke and ash to the air. Lack of sunlight would kill off plants and have a domino-like effect on other organisms in the food chain, including the dinosaurs.

It is possible that the reason for the dinosaurs' extinction may have been a combination of both theories. The dinosaurs may have been gradually declining, for whatever reason. The impact of a large object from space merely delivered the coup de grâce.

The fact that dinosaurs became extinct has been cited as proof of their inferiority and that they were evolutionary failures. However, these animals flourished for 150 million years. By comparison, the earliest ancestors of humanity appeared only about three million years ago. Humans have a long way to go before they can claim the same sort of success as the dinosaurs.

How did the **dodo** become extinct?

The dodo became extinct around 1800. Thousands were slaughtered for meat, but pigs and monkeys, which destroyed dodo eggs, were probably most responsible for the dodo's extinction. Dodos were native to the Mascarene Islands in the Central Indian Ocean. They became extinct on Mauritius soon after 1680 and on Réunion about 1750. They remained on Rodriguez until 1800.

What is a **quagga**?

The quagga, a native of South Africa, was basically a brown, rather than striped, zebra with white legs and tail. In the early 19th century, it lived in the wild in great herds **115**

When did the last passenger pigeon die?

At one time, 200 years ago, the passenger pigeon (*Ectopistes migratorius*) was the world's most abundant bird. Although the species was found only in eastern North America, it had a population of three to five billion birds (25% of the North American land bird population). Overhunting caused a chain of events that reduced their numbers below minimum threshold for viability. In the 1890s several states passed laws to protect the pigeon, but it was too late. The last known wild bird was shot in 1900. The last passenger pigeon, named Martha, died on September 1, 1914 in the Cincinnati Zoo.

and was tamed to become a harness animal or was killed for its skin. The species became extinct in 1883.

Under what conditions is a **species considered "endangered"**?

This determination is a complex process that has no set of fixed criteria that can be applied consistently to all species. The known number of living members in a species is not the sole factor. A species with a million members known to be alive but living in only one small area could be considered endangered, whereas another species having a smaller number of members, but spread out in a broad area, would not be considered so threatened. Reproduction data—the frequency of reproduction, the average number of offspring born, the survival rate, etc.—enter into such determinations. In the United States, the director of the U.S. Fish and Wildlife Service (within the Department of the Interior) determines which species are to be considered endangered, based on research and field data from specialists, biologists, botanists, and naturalists.

According to the Endangered Species Act of 1973, a species can be listed if it is threatened by any of the following:

1. The present or threatened destruction, modification, or curtailment of its habitat or range.

2. Utilization for commercial, sporting, scientific, or educational purposes at levels that detrimentally affect it.

3. Disease or predation.

4. Absence of regulatory mechanisms adequate to prevent the decline of a species or degradation of its habitat.

5. Other natural or man-made factors affecting its continued existence.

If the species is so threatened, the director then determines the "critical habitat," that is the species' inhabitation areas that contain the essential physical or biological features necessary for the species' preservation. The critical habitat can include non-habitation areas, which are deemed necessary for the protection of the species.

Which animal species have **become extinct** since the Endangered Species Act was passed in 1973, and which have subsequently **been removed from the list?**

Seven domestic species have been declared extinct: Florida's dusky seaside sparrow, the Santa Barbara song sparrow, the blue pike, the Tecopa pupfish, Sampson's pearly mussel, and the fishes the longjaw cisco and the Amistad gambusic.

Six species have been removed from the federal endangered and threatened species list since 1973 because they have recovered. Seven species have been removed from the federal list because they have become extinct.

How many species of **plants and animals** are **threatened** in the United States?

There are 206 threatened species (114 animals and 92 plants) in the United States; and 754 endangered species (320 animals and 434 plants).

Category	Threatened	Endangered	Threatened & Endangered
Mammals	9	55	64
Birds	16	74	90
Reptiles	19	14	33
Amphibians	5	7	12
Fishes	40	65	105
Snails	7	15	22
Clams	6	51	57
Crustaceans	3	14	17
Insects	9	20	29
Arachnids	0	5	5
Plants	92	434	526
TOTAL	206	754	960

What is the status of the **elephant** in Africa?

From 1979 to 1989, Africa lost half of its elephants from poaching and illegal ivory trade, with the population decreasing from an estimated 1.3 million to 600,000. This **117** led to the transfer of the African elephant from threatened to endangered status in October 1989 by CITES (the Convention on International Trade in Endangered Species). An ivory ban took effect on January 18, 1990; but six African countries (South Africa, Zimbabwe, Botswana, Namibia, Malawi, and Zambia) are trying to downlist this mammal to threatened status to allow them to trade in ivory again.

Altogether there are 35 African nations that have elephants, and all want to conserve this resource for their countries' benefit. Kenya now values a living elephant at $14,375 in tourism income for every year of its life, giving it a potential life-time value of $900,000. The ivory from an average elephant killed for its tusk would only be worth $1,000 (the price paid before the ban on ivory.

Are **turtles** endangered?

Worldwide turtle populations have declined due to several reasons, including habitat destruction; exploitation of species by humans for their eggs, leather, and meat; and their becoming accidently caught in the nets of fishermen. In particular danger are sea turtles, such as Kemp's ridley sea turtle (*Lepidochelys kempii*), which is believed to have a population of only a few hundred.

The endangered Kemp's ridley sea turtle.

What is the current population and status of the great whales?

Species	Latin Name	Original Population (thousands)	Current Population (thousands)	Status
Sperm	*Physeter macro cephalas*	2400	1974	Insufficient
Blue	*Balenoptera musculus*	226	13	Endangered
Finback	*Balenoptera physalus*	543	123	Vulnerable
Humpback	*Megaptera novaeangliae*	146	4	Vulnerable
Right	*Eubalaena glacialis*	120	3	Endangered
	Eubalaena australis			Vulnerable
Sei	*Balaenoptera borealis*	254	51	Vulnerable
Gray	*Eschrichtius robustus*	20	11	Unlisted
Bowhead	*Balaena mysticetus*	20	2	Vulnerable
Bryde's	*Balaenoptera edeni*	92	92	Insufficient
Minke	*Balaenoptera acutorostrata*	295	280	Insufficient

What is a **dolphin-safe tuna**?

The order Cetacea, composed of whales, dolphins, and porpoises, were spared from the extinction of large mammals at the end of the Pleistocene about 10,000 years ago. But from 1000 B.C.E. on they, especially the whale, have been relentlessly hunted by man for their valuable products. The twentieth century, with its many technological improvements, has become the most destructive period for the Cetacea. In 1972, the United States Congress passed the Marine Mammal Protection Act; one of its goals was to reduce the number of small cetaceans (notably *Stenalla* and *Delphinus*) killed and injured during commercial fishing operations, such as the incidental catch of dolphins in tuna purse-seines (nets that close up to form a huge ball to be hoisted aboard ship). Dolphins are often found swimming with schools of yellowfin tuna and are caught along with the tuna by fisherman who use purse-seine nets. The dolphins are drowned by this fishing method because they must be able to breathe air to survive. The number of incidental deaths and injuries in 1972 was estimated at 368,000 for United States fishing vessels and 55,078 for non–United States vessels. In 1979 the figures were reduced to 17,938 and 6,837 respectively. But in the 1980s, the dolphins killed by foreign vessels rose dramatically to over 100,000 a year. Most of the slaughter occurs in the eastern Pacific Ocean from Chile to Southern California.

To further reduce the numbers of dolphins killed during tuna catches, the three largest sellers of canned tuna in the United States, spearheaded by the Starkist company, decided that they would not sell tuna that has been caught by these methods harmful to dolphins. Only dolphin-safe tuna would be sold by them.

POLLUTION
See also: Health and Medicine—Health Hazards, Risks, Etc.

What is the **Pollutant Standard Index**?

The U.S. Environmental Protection Agency and the South Coast Air Quality Management District of El Monte, California, devised the Pollutant Standard Index to monitor concentrations of pollutants in the air and inform the public concerning related health effects. The scale measures the amount of pollution in parts per million, and has been in use nationwide since 1978.

PSI Index	Health Effects	Cautionary Status
0	Good	
50	Moderate	
100	Unhealthful	

119

PSI Index	Health Effects	Cautionary Status
200	Very unhealthful	Alert: elderly or ill should stay indoors and reduce physical activity.
300	Hazardous	Warning: General population should stay indoors and reduce physical activity.
400	Extremely hazardous	Emergency: all people remain indoors windows shut, no physical exertion.
500	Toxic	Significant harm; same as above.

What is the **Toxic Release Inventory (TRI)**?

TRI is a government mandated, publicly available compilation of information on the release of over 300 individual toxic chemicals and 20 categories of chemical compounds by manufacturing facilities in the United States. The law requires manufacturers to state the amounts of chemicals they release directly to air, land, or water, or that they transfer to off-site facilities that treat or dispose of wastes. The U.S. Environmental Protection Agency compiles these reports into an annual inventory and makes the information available in a computerized database. In 1992, 23,630 facilities released 3.2 billion pounds (1.5 billion kilograms) of toxic chemicals into the environment. Over 272 million pounds (124 million kilograms) of this total were released into surface water; 1.8 billion pounds (818 million kilograms) were emitted into the air; over 337 million pounds (153 million kilograms) were released to land; and over 725 million pounds (330 million kilograms) were injected into underground wells. The total amount of toxic chemicals released in 1992 was 6.6% lower than the amount released in 1991.

What are **PCBs**?

Polychlorinated biphenyls (PCBs) are a group of chemicals that were widely used before 1970 in the electrical industry, as a coolant for transformers and in capacitors and other electrical devices. They caused environmental problems because they do not break down, and can spread through the water, soil, and air. They have been linked by some scientists to cancer and reproductive disorders and have been shown to cause liver function abnormalities. Government action has resulted in the control of the use, disposal, and production of PCBs in nearly all areas of the world, including the United States.

What was the distribution of **radioactive fallout** after the 1986 Chernobyl accident?

Radioactive fallout, containing the isotope cesium 137, and nuclear contamination covered an enormous area, including Byelorussia, Latvia, Lithuania, the central portion of the then Soviet Union, the Scandinavian countries, the Ukraine, Poland, Austria, Czechoslovakia, Germany, Switzerland, northern Italy, eastern France, Romania, Bulgaria, Greece, Yugoslavia, the Netherlands, and the United Kingdom. The fallout, extremely uneven because of the shifting wind patterns, extended 1,200 to 1,300 miles (1,930 to 2,090 kilometers) from the point of the accident. Roughly 5% of the reactor fuel or seven tons of fuel containing 50 to 100 million curies were released. Estimates of the effects of this fallout range from 28,000 to 100,000 deaths from cancer and genetic defects within the next 50 years. In particular, livestock in high rainfall areas received unacceptable dosages of radiation.

How do **chlorofluorocarbons** affect the Earth's ozone layer?

Chlorofluorocarbons (CFCs) are hydrocarbons, such as freon, in which part or all of the hydrogen atoms have been replaced by fluorine atoms. These can be liquids or gases, are non-flammable and heat-stable, and are used as refrigerants, aerosol propellants, and solvents. When released into the air, they slowly rise into the Earth's upper atmosphere, where they are broken apart by ultraviolet rays from the sun. Some of the resultant molecular fragments react with the ozone in the atmosphere, reducing the amount of ozone. The CFC molecules' chlorine atoms act as catalysts in a complex set of reactions that convert two molecules of ozone into three molecules of ordinary hydrogen. This is depleting the beneficial ozone layer faster than it can be recharged by natural processes. The resultant "hole" lets through more ultraviolet light to the Earth's surface and creates health problems for humans, such as cataracts and skin cancer, and disturbs delicate ecosystems (for example, making plants produce less seed). In 1978 the United States government banned the use of fluorocarbon aerosols, and currently aerosol propellants have been changed from fluorocarbons to hydrocarbons, such as butane. Chemical industries must cut CFC manufacture to 50% by the year 2000; they have mounted a massive research effort to find a safer chemical substitute.

Since 1988 a substantial slowdown has taken place in the atmospheric buildup of two prime ozone-destroying compounds, CFC 11 and CFC 12. Based upon these measurements, experts suggest that concentrations of these CFCs will peak before the turn of the century, allowing the ozone layer to begin the slow process of repairing itself. It is believed that it will take 50 to 100 years for reactions in the atmosphere to reduce the concentrations of ozone-destroying chlorine and bromine back to natural levels. Until then, these chemicals will continue to erode the global ozone layer.

What are the components of **smog**?

Photochemical air pollution, commonly known as smog, is the result of a number of complex chemical reactions. The hydrocarbons, hydrocarbon derivations, and nitric oxides emitted from such sources as automobiles are the raw materials for photo- **121** chemical reactions. In the presence of oxygen and sunlight, the nitric oxides combine with organic compounds, such as the hydrocarbons from unburned gasoline, to produce a whitish haze, sometimes tinged with a yellow-brown color. In the process, a large number of new hydrocarbons and oxyhydrocarbons are produced. These secondary hydrocarbon products may compose as much as 95% of the total organics in a severe smog episode.

What are **flue gas "scrubbers"**?

The scrubbing of flue gases refers to the removal of sulfur dioxide (SO_2) and nitric oxide (NO), which are major components of air pollution. Wet scrubbers use a chemical solvent or lime, limestone, sodium alkali, or diluted sulfuric acid to remove the SO_2 formed during combustion. Dry scrubbing uses either a lime/limestone slurry or ammonia sprayed into the flue gases.

What is **acid rain**?

The term "acid rain" was coined by British chemist Robert Angus Smith (1817–1884) who, in 1872, published *Air & Rain: The Beginnings of a Chemical Climatology*. Since then, acid rain has unfortunately become an increasingly used term for rain, snow, sleet, or other precipitation that has been polluted by acids such as sulfuric and nitric acids.

When gasoline, coal, or oil are burned, their waste products of sulfur dioxide and nitrogen dioxide combine in complex chemical reactions with water vapor in clouds to form acids. The United States alone discharges 40 million metric tons of sulfur and nitrogen oxides into the atmosphere. This, combined with natural emissions of sulfur and nitrogen compounds, has resulted in severe ecological damage. Hundreds of lakes in North America (especially northeastern Canada and United States) and in Scandinavia are so acidic that they cannot support fish life. Crops, forests, and building materials, such as marble, limestone, sandstone, and bronze, have been affected as well, but the extent is not as well documented. However, in Europe, where so many living trees are stunted or killed, a new word *Waldsterben* (forest death) has been coined to describe this new phenomenon.

In 1990, amendments to the U.S. Clean Air Act contained provisions to control emissions that cause acid rain. It included the reductions of sulfur dioxide emissions from 19 million tons to 9.1 million tons annually and the reduction of industrial nitrogen oxide emissions from six to four million tons annually, both by the year 2000. Also the elimination of 90% of industrial benzene, mercury, and dioxin emissions, the reduction of automotive nitrogen oxide by 60%, and hydrocarbons by 40% by year 1997 were specified.

How **acidic** is acid rain?

Acidity or alkalinity is measured by a scale known as the pH (potential for Hydrogen) scale. It runs from zero to 14. Since it is logarithmic, a change in one unit equals a tenfold increase or decrease. So a solution at pH 2 is 10 times more acidic than one at pH 3 and 100 times as acidic as a solution at pH 4. Zero is extremely acid, 7 is neutral, and 14 is very alkaline. Any rain below 5.0 is considered acid rain; some scientists use the value of 5.6 or less. Normal rain and snow containing dissolved carbon dioxide (a weak acid) measure about pH 5.6. Actual values vary according to geographical area. Eastern Europe and parts of Scandinavia have 4.3 to 4.5; the rest of Europe is 4.5 to 5.1; eastern United States and Canada ranges from 4.2 to 4.6, and Mississippi Valley has a range of 4.6 to 4.8. The worst North American area, having 4.2, is centered around Lake Erie and Lake Ontario. For comparison, some common items and their pH values are listed below:

Concentrated sulfuric acid	1.0
Lemon juice	2.3
Vinegar	3.3
Acid rain	4.3
Normal rain	5.0 to 5.6
Normal lakes and rivers	5.6 to 8.0
Distilled water	7.0
Human blood	7.35 to 7.45
Seawater	7.6 to 8.4

How much **oil** is **dumped into the oceans**?

Every year well over three million metric tons of oil contaminate the sea. A half comes from ships, but the rest come from land-based pollution, with only 33% of it spilled by accident. More than 1.1 million metric tons of oil are deliberately discharged from tankers washing out their tanks.

Source of oil	% of total
Tankers operational discharge	22%
Municipal wastes	22%
Tanker accidents	12.5%
Atmospheric rainout (oil released by industry and cars)	9.5%
Bilge and fuel oils	9%
Natural seeps	7.5%
Non-refining industrial waste	6%
Urban runoff	3.5%
Coastal oil refineries	3%
Offshore production	1.5%
River runoff	1%
Others	2.5%

Where did the **first major oil spill** occur?

The first major commercial oil spill occurred on March 18, 1967, when the tanker *Torrey Canyon* grounded on the Seven Stones Shoal off the coast of Cornwall, England, spilling 830,000 barrels (119,000 tons) of Kuwaiti oil into the sea. This was the first major tanker accident. However during World War II, German U-boat attacks on tankers, between January and June of 1942, off the United States East Coast, spilled 590,000 tons of oil. Although the *Exxon Valdez* was widely publicized as a major spill of 35,000 tons in 1989, it is dwarfed by the deliberate dumping of oil from Sea Island into the Persian Gulf on January 25, 1991. It is estimated that the spill equaled almost 1.5 million tons of oil. A major spill also occurred in Russia in October 1994 in the Komi region of the Arctic. The size of the spill was reported to be as much as two million barrels (286,000 tons).

In addition to the large disasters, day-to-day pollution occurs from drilling platforms where waste generated from platform life, including human waste, and oils, chemicals, mud and rock from drilling are discharged into the water.

Date	Cause	Thousands tons spilled
1/42-6/42	German U-boat attacks on tankers off the East Coast of U.S. during World War II	590
3/18/67	Tanker Torrey Canyon grounds off Land's End in the English Channel	119
3/20/70	Tanker Othello collides with another ship in Tralhavet Bay, Sweden	60–100
12/19/72	Tanker Sea Star collides with another ship in Gulf of Oman	115
5/12/76	Urquiola grounds at La Coruna, Spain	100
3/16/78	Tanker Amoco Cadiz grounds off Northwest France	223
6/3/79	Itox I oil well blows in Southern Gulf of Mexico	600
7/79	Tankers Atlantic Express and Aegean Captain collide off Trinidad and Tobago	300
2/19/83	Blowout in Norwuz oil field in the Persian Gulf	600
8/6/83	Fire aboard Castillo de Beliver off Cape Town, South Africa	250
1/25/91	Iraq begins deliberately dumping oil into Persian Gulf from Sea Island, Kuwait	1,450

How harmful are balloon releases?

Both latex and metallic balloons can be harmful. A latex balloon can land in water, lose its color, and resemble a jellyfish, which if eaten by sea animals can cause their death because they cannot digest it. A metal balloon can get caught in electric wires and cause power outages.

What are **Operation Ranch Hand** and **Agent Orange**?

Operation Ranch Hand was the tactical military project for the aerial spraying of herbicides in South Vietnam during the Vietnam Conflict (1961–1975). In these operations Agent Orange, the collective name for the herbicides 2,4-D and 2,4,5-T, was used for the defoliation. The name derives from the color-coded drums in which the herbicides were stored. In all, U.S. troops sprayed approximately 19 million gallons (72 million liters) of herbicides over four million acres (1.6 million hectare).

Concerns about the health effects of Agent Orange were initially voiced in 1970, and since then the issue has been complicated by scientific and political debate. In 1993, a 16-member panel of experts reviewed the existing scientific evidence and found strong evidence of a statistical association between herbicides and soft-tissue sarcoma, non-Hodgkin's lymphoma, Hodgkin's disease and chloracne. On the other hand, they concluded that no connection appeared to exist between exposure to Agent Orange and skin cancer, bladder cancer, brain tumors, or stomach cancer.

What causes **formaldehyde contamination** in homes?

Formaldehyde contamination is related to the widespread construction use of wood products bonded with urea-formaldehyde resins and products containing formaldehyde. Major formaldehyde sources include subflooring of particle board; wall paneling made from hardwood plywood or particle board; and cabinets and furniture made from particle board, medium density fiberboard, hardwood plywood, or solid wood. Urea-formaldehyde foam insulation (UFFI) has received the most media notoriety and regulatory attention. Formaldehyde is also used in drapes, upholstery, carpeting, and wallpaper adhesives, milk cartons, car bodies, household disinfectants, permanent-press clothing, and paper towels. In particular, mobile homes seem to have higher formaldehyde levels than houses do. Six billion pounds (2.7 billion kilograms) of formaldehyde are used in the United States each year.

The release of formaldehyde into the air by these products (called outgassing) can develop poisoning symptoms in humans. The EPA classifies formaldehyde as a potential human carcinogen (cancer-causing agent).

Which pollutants lead to **indoor air pollution**?

Indoor air pollution, also known as "tight building syndrome," results from conditions in modern, high energy efficiency buildings, which have reduced outside air exchange, or have inadequate ventilation, chemical contamination, and microbial contamination. Indoor air pollution can produce various symptoms, such as headache, nausea, and eye, nose, and throat irritation. In addition houses are affected by indoor air pollution emanating from consumer and building products and from tobacco smoke. Below are listed some pollutants found in houses:

Pollutant	Sources	Effects
Asbestos	Old or damaged insulation, fireproofing, or acoustical tiles	Many years later, chest and abdominal cancers and lung diseases
Biological pollutants	Bacteria, mold and mildew, viruses, animal dander and cat saliva, mites, cockroaches, and pollen	Eye, nose, and throat irritation; shortness of breath; dizziness; lethargy; fever; digestive problems; asthma; influenza and other infectious diseases
Carbon monoxide	Unvented kerosene and gas heaters; leaking chimneys and furnaces; wood stoves and fireplaces; gas stoves; automobile exhaust from attached garages; tobacco smoke	At low levels, fatigue; at higher levels, impaired vision and coordination; headaches; dizziness; confusion; nausea. Fatal at very high concentrations
Formaldehyde	Plywood, wall paneling, particle board, fiber-board; foam insulation; fire and tobacco smoke; textiles, and glues	Eye, nose, and throat irritations; wheezing and coughing; fatigue; skin rash; severe allergic reactions; may cause cancer
Lead	Automobile exhaust; sanding or burning of lead paint; soldering	Impaired mental and physical development in children; decreased coordination and mental abilities; kidneys, nervous system, and red blood cells damage

Pollutant	Sources	Effects
Mercury	Some latex paints	Vapors can cause kidney damage; long–term exposure can cause brain damage
Nitrogen dioxide	Kerosene heaters, unvented gas stoves and heaters; tobacco smoke	Eye, nose, and throat irritation; may impair lung function and increase respiratory infections in young children
Organic Gases	Paints, paint strippers, solvents, wood preservatives; aerosol sprays; cleansers and disinfectants; moth repellents; air fresheners; stored fuels; hobby supplies; dry-cleaned clothing.	Eye, nose and throat irritation; headaches; loss of coordination; nausea; damage to liver, kidney, and nervous system; some organics cause cancer in animals and are suspected of causing cancer in humans.
Pesticides	Products used to kill household pests and products used on lawns or gardens that drift or are tracked inside the house.	Irritation to eye, nose, and throat; damage to nervous system and kidneys; cancer.
Radon	Earth and rock beneath the home; well water, building materials.	No immediate symptoms; estimated to cause about 10% of lung cancer deaths; smokers at higher risk.

RECYCLING, CONSERVATION, AND WASTE

See also: Energy—Consumption and Conservation

What is the **NIMBY** syndrome?

NIMBY is the acronym for "Not In My Back Yard," referring to major community resistance to new incinerator sitings, landfills, prisons, roads, etc. NIMFY is "Not In My Front Yard."

Which states have the greatest number of **hazardous waste sites**?

The top five are:

New Jersey	107
Pennsylvania	102
New York	81
California	96
Michigan	77

A total of 1,276 sites were recorded.

Where are the six **nuclear dump sites** in the United States?

As of 1991, the six nuclear waste dump sites are in West Valley, New York; Sheffield, Illinois; Maxey Flats, Kentucky; Barnwell, South Carolina; Beatty, Nevada; and Richland, Washington.

How is **nuclear waste** stored?

Nuclear wastes consist either of fission products formed from atom splitting of uranium, cesium, strontium, or krypton, or from transuranic elements formed when uranium atoms absorb free neutrons. Wastes from transuranic elements are less radioactive than fission products; however, these elements remain radioactive far longer— hundreds of thousands of years. The types of waste are irradiated fuel (spent fuel) in the form of 12-foot (4-meter) long rods, high-level radioactive waste in the form of liquid or sludge, and low-level waste (non-transuranic or legally high-level) in the form of reactor hardware, piping, toxic resins, water from fuel pool, etc.

In the United States most of the spent fuel has been left for 10 years or more in water-filled pools at the individual plant sites. They are waiting permanent disposal that is set for 1998 by a mandate in the Nuclear Waste Policy Act (1982). Most low-level radioactive waste has been stored in steel drums in shallow landfills at the six nuclear dump sites and at the Hanford Nuclear Reservation in the state of Washington. Most high-level nuclear waste has been stored in double-walled stainless-steel tanks surrounded by three feet (one meter) of concrete. The current best storage method, developed by the French in 1978, is to incorporate the waste into a special molten glass mixture, then enclose it in a steel container and bury it in a special pit.

How much **garbage** does the average American generate?

According to one study, Americans produce about 230 million tons of refuse a year—
128 5.1 pounds (2.3 kilograms) per person a day or about 1,900 pounds (863 kilograms)

per year. Another survey reported that a typical suburban family of three generated 40 pounds (18 kilograms) of garbage weekly with the components of the content given in percentages below:

Type of solid waste	Percent
Aluminum	1%
Polystyrene meat trays, cups, egg cartons, and packing	3%
Disposable diapers	3%
Wood, textiles, old clothing	5%
Metal cans and nails	5%
Plastic soda bottles and bags	5%
Glass	8%
Miscellaneous	10%
Food	11%
Paper	21%
Yard waste and grass clippings	23%

An analysis by the U.S. Environmental Protection Agency, published in 1990, indicated not only an increase in the amount of garbage per person, but a change in the content of it as well:

Garbage in pounds per person per day				
Waste materials	1960	1970	1980	1988
Total nonfood product wastes	1.65	2.26	2.57	2.94
Paper and paperboard	0.91	1.19	1.32	1.60
Glass	0.20	0.34	0.36	0.28
Metals	0.32	0.38	0.35	0.34
Plastics	0.01	0.08	0.19	0.32
Rubber and leather	0.06	0.09	0.10	0.10
Textiles	0.05	0.05	0.06	0.09
Wood	0.09	0.11	0.12	0.14
Other	0.00	0.02	0.07	0.07
Other Wastes				
Food wastes	0.37	0.34	0.32	0.29
Yard wastes	0.61	0.62	0.66	0.70
Miscellaneous inorganic waste	0.04	0.05	0.05	0.06
Total waste generated	2.66	3.27	3.61	4.00

How much **solid waste** is generated annually in the United States?

The United States produces 4.543 million tons of solid waste annually.

Type of waste	Million tons	Percent
Agriculture	2,340	52
Mineral industries (mining and milling waste)	1,620	36
Industrial (nonhazardous)	225	5
Municipal (domestic)	180	4
Utility	90	2
Hazardous	45	2
Low-level radioactive	3	0.0007

Of the municipal solid wastes in 1988 of approximately 180 million tons in the above table, paper waste ranked the highest.

Municipal Solid Waste	
Type of waste	Million tons
Paper	71.8
Yard wastes	31.6
Rubber, Textile, Wood, etc.	20.8
Metals	15.3
Plastics	14.4
Food wastes	13.2
Glass	12.5

How critical is the problem of **landfilling** in the United States?

According to one source, landfilling is currently over-used in the United States, but will continue to be an essential component of waste management. There are more than 9,000 landfills in the United States. In 1960, 62% of all garbage was sent to landfills; in 1980, the figure was 81%; and in 1990 it decreased to 67%. After as much waste as possible has been reduced, recovered, reused, or converted to energy, there will still be some waste that cannot be disposed of in any other way except in landfills. However, landfill capacity is already dwindling severely in the most populous regions of the country. In 1995, a study reported that the number of landfills accepting municipal solid waste had declined from 4,482 to 3,558.

How much does **packaging** contribute to municipal solid waste?

Packaging accounted for 30.3% of municipal solid waste in 1990. The material components of this figure are paper (47.7%), glass (24.5%), plastic (14.5%), steel (6.5%), wood (4.5%), and aluminum (2.3%).

How much space does a **recycled ton of paper** save in a landfill?

Each ton (907 kilograms) saves more than three cubic yards of landfill space.

What **natural resources** are saved by **recycling paper**?

One ton (907 kilograms) of recycled waste paper would save an average of 7,000 gallons (26,460 liters) of water, 3.3 cubic yards (2.5 cubic meters) of landfill space, three barrels of oil, 17 trees, and 4,000 kilowatt-hours of electricity, or energy to power the average home for six months.

How much **newspaper** must be recycled to **save one tree**?

One 35 to 40 foot (10.6 to 12 meter) tree produces a stack of newspapers four feet (1.2 meters) thick; this much newspaper must be recycled to save a tree.

How much **waste paper** does a **newspaper** generate?

An average yearly newspaper subscription (for example *The San Francisco Chronicle*) received every day, produces 550 pounds (250 kilograms) of waste paper (per subscription per year). The average *New York Times* Sunday edition produces eight million pounds (3.6 million kilograms) of waste paper.

How many **paper mills** in the United States use waste paper to produce new products?

Of the approximately 600 mills in the United States producing pulp, paper, paperboard, or building products, 200 depend almost entirely on waste paper for their raw material. Another 300 mills use 10% to 50% waste paper in their manufacturing processes.

What problems may be encountered when **polyvinyl chloride (PVC) plastics** are burned?

Chlorinated plastics, such as PVC, contribute to the formation of hydrochloric acid gases. They also may be a part of a mix of substances containing chlorine that form a precursor to dioxin in the burning process. Polystyrene, polyethylene, and polyethylene terephthalate (PET) do not produce these pollutants.

What do the **numbers** inside the **recycling symbol** on plastic containers mean?

The Society of the Plastics Industry developed a voluntary coding system for plastic containers to assist recyclers in sorting plastic containers. The symbol is designed to be imprinted on the bottom of the plastic containers. The numerical code appears inside a three-sided triangular arrow. A guide to what the numbers mean is listed below. The most commonly recycled plastics are polyethylene terephthalate (PET) and high density polyethylene (HDPE).

Code	Material	Examples
1	Polyethylene terephthalate (PET)	Soft drink bottles
2	High-density polyethylene (HDPE)	Milk and water jugs
3	Vinyl	Shampoo bottles
4	Low-density polyethylene (LDPE)	Ketchup bottles
5	Polypropylene	Squeeze bottles
6	Polystyrene	Fast-food packaging
7	Other	

What products are made from **recycled plastic**?

Resin	Common Uses	Products Made From Recycled Resin
HDPE	Beverage bottles, milk jugs, milk and soft drink crates, pipe, cable, film	Motor oil bottles, detergent bottles, pipes and pails
LDPE	Film bags such as trash bags, coatings, and plastic bottles.	New trash bags, pallets
PET	Soft drink, detergent, and juice bottles	Carpets, fiberfill, non-food bottles/containers
PP	Auto battery cases, screw-on caps and lids; some yogurt and margarine tubs, plastic film	Auto parts, batteries, carpets
PS	Housewares, electronics, fast food carry-out packaging, plastic utensils	Insulation board, office equipment, reusable cafeteria trays
PVC	Sporting goods, luggage, pipes, auto parts. In packaging for shampoo bottles, blister packaging, and films	Drainage pipes, fencing, house siding

    A new clothing fiber called Fortrel EcoSpun is made from recycled plastic soda bottles. The fiber is knit or woven into garments such as fleece for outerwear or long

---

Are cloth diapers or disposable diapers better for the environment?

This is a complex matter with both alternatives having an environmental impact. Disposable diapers make up 2% of the total solid waste while cloth diapers account for only 1% of the solid waste. In 1990, 16 to 17 billion disposable diapers were sold. However, cleaning cloth diapers requires the use of detergents (polluting-agent) and hot water (energy user). In addition, if a professional diaper service is used, then there is extra gasoline for delivery and the exhaust from trucks contributes to air pollution.

---

underwear. The processor estimates that every pound of Fortrel EcoSpun fiber results in 10 plastic bottles being kept out of landfills.

Is **washing dishes by hand** better for the environment than using an automatic **dishwasher**?

Dishwashers often save energy and water compared to hand washing. Depending on the brand, dishwashers typically consume 7.5 to 12 gallons (28 to 45 liters) of water per normal wash. Hand-washing a day's worth of dishes may use up to 15 gallons (57 liters) of water. One university study found that dishwashers consume about 37% less water than washing by hand.

Several steps can be taken for additional energy savings when using a dishwasher. The setting on a home's water heater can be turned down to 120°F (49°C) if the dishwasher has a booster heater. While some machines feature no-heat air-dry setting, simply opening the door after the final rinse to let the dishes air dry will save energy. Prewashing the dishes before loading generally wastes water since most machines can handle even heavily soiled plates.

How many **automobile tires** are scrapped each year and what can be done with them?

Approximately 242 million tires are discarded annually in the United States. Less than 7% are recycled, 11% are burned for their fuel value, and 5% are exported. The remaining 78% are sent to landfills, stockpiled, or illegally dumped.

A major use for discarded tires is in rubber modified asphalt and concrete. They can also be recycled into new products such as floor mats, blasting mats, and muffler hangers. Tires that have been ground into crumb can be used in a variety of molded or **133** die cut products such as traffic cone bases, mud flaps, and moisture barriers. Whole tires can be used in artificial reefs, for erosion control and to stabilize mine tailing ponds.

What is a **WOBO**?

A WOBO (world bottle) is the first mass-produced container designed for secondary use as a building product. It was conceived by Albert Heineken of the Heineken beer family. The beer bottles were designed in a special shape to be used, when empty, as glass bricks for building houses. The actual building carried out with WOBOs was only a small shed and a double garage built on the Heineken estate at Noordwijk, near Amsterdam. Although not implemented, WOBO was a sophisticated and intelligent design solution to what has emerged as a major environmental issue in recent years.

BIOLOGY

EVOLUTION AND GENETICS

Which **biological events** occurred during the **geologic time divisions**?

		Cenozoic Era (Age of Mammals)		
Period	**Epoch**	**Beginning date in est. millions of years**	**Plants and microorganisms**	**Animals**
Quaternary	Holocene (Recent)	10,000 years ago	Decline of woody plants and rise of herbaceous plants	Age of *Homo sapiens*; humans dominate
	Pleistocene	1.9	Extinction of many species (from 4 ice ages)	Extinction of many large mammals (from 4 ice ages)
Tertiary	Pliocene	6.0	Development of grass-lands; decline of forests; flowering plants	Large carnivores; many grazing mammals; first known human-like primates
	Miocene	25.0		Many modern mammals evolve

Cenozoic Era
(Age of Mammals)

Period	Epoch	Beginning date in est. millions of years	Plants and microorganisms	Animals
Tertiary	Oligocene	38.0	Spread of forests; flowering plants, rise of monocotyledons	Apes evolve; all present mammal families evolve; saber-toothed cats
	Eocene	55.0	Gymnosperms and angiosperms dominant	Beginning of age of mammals; modern birds
	Paleocene	65.0		Evolution of primate mammals

Mesozoic Era
(Age of Reptiles)

Period	Epoch	Beginning date in est. millions of years	Plants and microorganisms	Animals
Cretaceous		135.0	Rise of angiosperms; gymnosperms decline	Dinosaurs reach peak and then become extinct; toothed birds become extinct; first modern birds; primitive mammals
Jurassic		200.0	Ferns and gymnosperms common	Large, specialized dinosaurs; insectivorous marsupials
Triassic		250.0	Gymnosperms and ferns dominate	First dinosaurs; egg-laying mammals.

Paleozic Era
(Age of Ancient Life)

Period	Epoch	Beginning date in est. millions of years	Plants and microorganisms	Animals
Permian		285.0	Conifers evolve.	Modern insects appear; mammal-

Period	Epoch	Beginning date in est. millions of years	Plants and microorganisms	Animals
				like reptiles; extinction of many Paleozic invertebrates
Carboniferous (divided into Mississippian and Pennsylvanian periods by some in the U.S.)		350.0	Forests of ferns and gymnosperms; swamps; club mosses and horsetails	Ancient sharks abundant; many echinoderms, mollusks and insect forms; first reptiles; spread of ancient amphibians
Devonian		410.0	Terrestrial plants established; first forests; gymnosperms appear	Age of fish; amphibians; wingless insects and millipedes appear
Silurian		425.0	Vascular plants appear; algae dominant	Fish evolve; marine arachnids dominant; first insects; crustaceans
Ordovician		500.0	Marine algae dominant; terrestrial plants first appear	Invertebrates dominant; first fish appear
Cambrian		570.0	Algae dominant	Age of marine invertebrates

Precambrian Era

Period	Epoch	Beginning date in est. millions of years	Plants and microorganisms	Animals
Archeozoic and Proterozoic Eras		3800.0	Bacterial cells; then primitive algae and fungi; marine protozoans	Marine invertebrates at end of period
Azoic		4600.0	Origin of the Earth.	

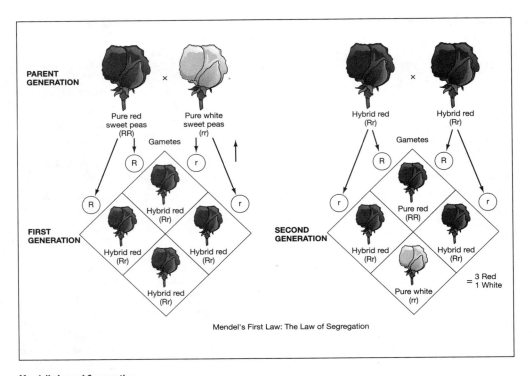

PARENT GENERATION

Pure red sweet peas (RR)

Pure white sweet peas (rr)

Gametes

R   r

R   r

FIRST GENERATION

Hybrid red (Rr)

Hybrid red (Rr)   Hybrid red (Rr)

Hybrid red (Rr)

Hybrid red (Rr)   Hybrid red (Rr)

Hybrid red (Rr)

Gametes

R   R

SECOND GENERATION

r   r

Pure red (RR)

Hybrid red (Rr)   Hybrid red (Rr)

Pure white (rr)

= 3 Red 1 White

Mendel's First Law: The Law of Segregation

Mendel's Law of Segregation.

How did **humans evolve**?

Evolution of the *Homo* lineage of modern humans (*Homo sapiens*) began with the hunter of nearly five feet tall, *Homo habilis*, who is widely presumed to have evolved from an australopithecine ancestor. Near the beginning of the Pleistocene (two million years ago), *Homo habilis* was transformed into *Homo erectus* (Java Man), who used fire and possessed culture. Middle Pleistocene populations of *Homo erectus* are said to show steady evolution toward the anatomy of *Homo sapiens* (Neanderthals, Cro-Magnons, and modern humans), 120,000 to 40,000 years ago. Pre-modern *Homo sapiens* built huts and made clothing.

What is meant by **Mendelian inheritance**?

Mendelian inheritance refers to genetic traits carried through heredity; the process was studied and described by Austrian monk Gregor Mendel (1822–1889). Mendel was the first to deduce correctly the basic principles of heredity. Mendelian traits are also called single gene or monogenic traits, because they are controlled by the action of a single gene or gene pair. More than 4,300 human disorders are known or suspected to be inherited as Mendelian traits, encompassing autosomal dominant (e.g., neurofibromatosis), autosomal recessive (e.g., cystic fibrosis), sex-linked dominant and recessive conditions (e.g., color-blindness and hemophilia).

Overall, incidence of Mendelian disorders in the human population is about 1%. Many non-anomalous characteristics that make up human variation are also inherited in Mendelian fashion.

Who is generally known as the **founder of genetics**?

Gregor Mendel (1822–1884), an Austrian monk and biologist, is considered the founder of genetics. Using his knowledge of statistics to analyze biological phenomena, Mendel discovered specific and regular ratios that he used to formulate the laws of heredity. It was the English biologist William Bateson (1861–1926), however, who brought Mendel's work to the attention of the scientific world and who coined the term "genetics."

What is the significance of *On the Origin of Species*?

Charles Darwin.

Charles Darwin (1809–1882) first proposed a theory of evolution based on natural selection in his treatise *On the Origin of Species*. The publication of *On the Origin of Species* ushered in a new era in our thinking about the nature of man. The intellectual revolution it caused and the impact it had on man's concept of himself and the world were greater than those caused by the works of Newton and others. The effect was immediate, the first edition being sold out on the day of publication (November 24, 1859). *Origin* has been referred to as "the book that shook the world." Every modern discussion of man's future, the population explosion, the struggle for existence, the purpose of man and the universe, and man's place in nature rests on Darwin.

The work was a product of his analyses and interpretations of his findings from his voyages on the H.M.S. *Beagle*, as a naturalist. In Darwin's day, the prevailing explanation for organic diversity was the story of creation in the book of Genesis in the Bible. *Origin* was the first publication to present scientifically sound, well-organized evidence for evolution. Darwin's theory of evolution was based on natural selection in which the best, the fittest, survive, and if there is a difference in genetic endowment **139** among individuals, the race will, by necessity, steadily improve. It is a two-step process: the first consists of the production of variation, and the second, of the sorting of this variability by natural selection in which the favorable variations tend to be preserved.

Did Charles Darwin have any nicknames?

Darwin had several nicknames. As a young naturalist on board the H.M.S. *Beagle*, he was called "Philos" because of his intellectual pursuits and "Flycatcher" when his shipmates tired of him filling the ship with his collections. Later in his life, when he became a leader in the scientific community, journalists refered to him as "The Sage of Down" or "The Saint of Science," but his friend Thomas Henry Huxley privately called him "The Czar of Down" and the "Pope of Science." His own favorite nickname was "Stultis the Fool" and he often signed letters to scientific friends with "Stultis." This name referred to his habit of trying experiments most people would prejudge to be fruitless or fool's experiments.

Who coined the phrase "survival of the fittest"?

Although frequently associated with Darwinism, this phrase was coined by Herbert Spencer (1820–1903), an English sociologist. It is the process by which organisms that are less well-adapted to their environment tend to perish and better-adapted organisms tend to survive.

What is Batesian mimicry?

In 1861, Henry Walter Bates (1825–1892), a British naturalist, proposed that a non-toxic species can evolve (especially in color and color pattern) to look like a toxic or unpalatable species, or to act like a toxic species, to avoid being eaten by a predator. The classic example is the viceroy butterfly, which resembles the unpalatable monarch butterfly. This is called Batesian mimicry. Subsequently, Fritz Müller (1821–1897), a German-born zoologist, discovered that all the species of similar appearance become distasteful to predators. This phenomenon is called Müllerian mimicry.

When was the Scopes (monkey) trial?

John T. Scopes (1900–1970), a high-school biology teacher, was brought to trial by the State of Tennessee in 1925 for teaching the theory of evolution. He challenged a recent law passed by the Tennessee legislature that made it unlawful to teach in any public school any theory that denies the divine creation of man. He was convicted and sentenced, but the decision was reversed later and the law repealed in 1967.

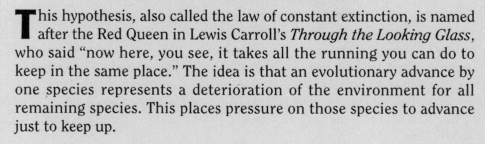

What is the Red Queen hypothesis?

This hypothesis, also called the law of constant extinction, is named after the Red Queen in Lewis Carroll's *Through the Looking Glass*, who said "now here, you see, it takes all the running you can do to keep in the same place." The idea is that an evolutionary advance by one species represents a deterioration of the environment for all remaining species. This places pressure on those species to advance just to keep up.

At the present, pressure against school boards still affects the teaching of evolution. Recent drives by anti-evolutionists either have tried to ban the teaching of evolution or have demanded "equal time" for "special creation" as described in the biblical book of Genesis. This has raised many questions about the separation of church and state, the teaching of controversial subjects in public schools, and the ability of scientists to communicate with the public. The gradual improvement of the fossil record, the result of comparative anatomy, and many other developments in biological science contributed toward making evolutionary thinking more palatable.

What is **genetic engineering**?

Genetic engineering is the deliberate alteration of the genetic make-up (genome) of an organism by manipulation of its DNA (deoxyribonucleic acid) molecule (a double helix chemical structure containing genetic information) to effect a change in heredity traits.

Genetic engineering techniques include cell fusion and the use of recombinant DNA (RNA) or gene-splicing. In cell fusion, the tough outer membranes of sperm and egg cells are stripped off by enzymes, and then the fragile cells are mixed and combined with the aid of chemicals or viruses. The result may be the creation of a new life form from two species. Recombinant DNA techniques transfer a specific genetic activity from one organism to the next through the use of bacterial plasmids (small circular pieces of DNA lying outside the main bacterial chromosome) and enzymes, such as restriction endonucleases (which cut the DNA strands); reverse transcriptase (which makes a DNA strand from an RNA strand); DNA ligase (which joins DNA strands together); and tag polymerase (which can make a double-stranded DNA molecule from a single stranded "primer" molecule). The process begins with the isolation of suitable DNA strands and fragmenting them. After these fragments are combined with vectors, they are carried into bacterial cells where the DNA fragments are "spliced" on to plasmid DNA that has been opened up. These hybrid plasmids are now mixed with host **141** cells to form transformed cells. Since only some of the transformed cells will exhibit the desired characteristic or gene activity, the transformed cells are separated and grown individually in cultures. This methodology has been successful in producing large quantities of hormones (such as insulin) for the biotechnology industry. However, it is more difficult to transform animal and plant cells. Yet the technique exists to make plants resistant to diseases and to make animals grow larger. Because genetic engineering interferes with the processes of heredity and can alter the genetic structure of our own species, there is much concern over the ethical ramifications of such power, as well as the possible health and ecological consequences of the creation of these bacterial forms. Some applications of genetic engineering in the various fields are listed below:

Agriculture—Crops having larger yields, disease- and drought-resistancy; bacterial sprays to prevent crop damage from freezing temperatures (1987); and livestock improvement through changes in animal traits (1982).

Industry—Use of bacteria to convert old newspaper and wood chips into sugar; oil- and toxin-absorbing bacteria for oil spill or toxic waste clean-ups (1991); and yeasts to accelerate wine fermentation.

Medicine—Alteration of human genes to eliminate disease (1990, experimental stage); faster and more economical production of vital human substances to alleviate deficiency and disease symptoms (but not to cure them) such as insulin (1982), interferon (cancer therapy), vitamins, human growth hormone ADA (1990), antibodies, vaccines, and antibiotics.

Research—Modification of gene structure in medical research (1989), especially cancer research (1990).

Food processing—Rennin (enzyme) in cheese aging (1989).

What is the **Genome Project**?

In late 1990, the biomedical community began work on a 15-year, $3 billion (government-financed) program to map the entire human *genome* (the complete genetic structure), which contains 50,000 to 100,000 genes. So far, 2,000 genes have been identified and mapped. The goal is not only to pinpoint these genes, but also to decode the biochemical information down to the so called "letters" of inheritance, the four basic constituents of all genes called *nucleotides*: A (adenine), C (cytosine), G (guanine), and T (thymine). Since these letters are linked in pairs of sequences in the double helix of DNA, this means that three billion pairs are involved in this process. The knowledge gained from the project would be a basis for studying human diseases, understanding evolution, and accelerating biomedical research. Although there is some controversy about spending such a large sum of money on one project, steady progress is being made in completing the program.

Can **human beings** be **cloned**?

In theory, yes. There are, however, many technical obstacles to human cloning, as well as moral, ethical, philosophical, religious, and economic issues to be resolved before a human being could be cloned.

A clone is a group of cells derived from the original cell by fission (one cell dividing into two cells) or by mitosis (cell nucleus division with each chromosome splitting into two). It perpetuates an existing organism's genetic make-up. Gardeners have been making clones (copies) of plants for centuries by taking cuttings of plants to make genetically identical copies. For plants that refuse to grow from cuttings, or for the animal world, modern scientific techniques have greatly extended the range of cloning. The technique for plants starts with taking a cutting of a plant, usually the "best" one in terms of reproductivity or decorativeness or other standard. Since all the plant's cells contain the genetic information from which the entire plant can be reconstructed, the cutting can be taken from any part of the plant. Placed in a culture medium having nutritious chemicals and a growth hormone, the cells in the cutting divide, doubling in size every six weeks until the mass of cells produces small white globular points called embryoids. These embryoids develop roots, or shoots, and begin to look like tiny plants. Transplanted into compost, these plants grow into exact copies of the parent plant. The whole process takes 18 months. This process, called tissue culture, has been used to make clones of oil palm, asparagus, pineapples, strawberries, brussels sprouts, cauliflower, bananas, carnations, ferns, etc. Besides making high productive copies of the best plant available, this method controls viral diseases that are passed through seed generations.

For animals, a technique called nuclear transfer enables up to 32 clones to be produced at one time. An embryo at the 32-cell stage of development is split up using tiny surgical tools. Each of the 32 cells then are combined with single cell embryos (from the same species) from which the nucleus has been removed. This method has been used on mice, frogs, sheep, and cattle. Ultimately, there seems to be no biological reason why human beings could not be cloned, sometime in the future.

Who originated the idea called **panspermia**?

Panspermia is the idea that microorganisms, spores, or bacteria attached to tiny particles of matter have traveled through space, eventually landing on a suitable planet and initiated the rise of life there. The word itself means "all-seeding." The British scientist Lord Kelvin (1824–1907) suggested, in the 19th century, that life may have arrived here from outer space, perhaps carried by meteorites. In 1903, the Swedish chemist Svante Arrhenius (1859–1927) put forward the more complex panspermia idea that life on Earth was "seeded" by means of extraterrestrial spores, bacteria, and microorganisms coming here on tiny bits of cosmic matter.

What is the difference between **DNA** and **RNA**?

DNA (deoxyribonucleic acid) is a nucleic acid formed from a repetition of simple building blocks called nucleotides. The nucleotides consist of phosphate (PO_4), sugar (deoxyribose) and a base that is either adenine (A), thymine (T), guanine (G), or cytosine (C). In a DNA molecule, this basic unit is repeated in a double helix structure made from two chains of nucleotides linked between the bases. The links are either between A and T or between G and C. The structure of the bases does not allow other kinds of links. The famous double helix structure resembles a twisted ladder. The 1962 Nobel Prize in physiology or medicine was awarded to James Watson (b. 1928), Francis Crick (b. 1916), and Maurice Wilkins (b. 1916) for determining the molecular structure of DNA.

RNA (ribonucleic acid) is also a nucleic acid, but it consists of a single chain and the sugar is ribose rather than deoxyribose. The bases are the same except that the thymine (T) which appears in DNA is replaced by another base called uracil (U), which links only to adenine (A).

How much **DNA** is in a typical human cell?

If the DNA in a single human cell were stretched out and laid end-to-end, it would measure approximately 6.5 feet (two meters). The average human body contains 10 to 20 billion miles (16 to 32 billion kilometers) of DNA distributed among trillions of cells.

What is **antisense**?

Antisense molecules, which are microscopic bits of DNA or RNA, are designed to bind to a cell's own DNA or RNA and interfere with its activity. It is hoped that antisense drugs can slow the progression of some types of cancer.

What is **p53**?

Discovered in 1979, *p53* is a gene that, when a cell's DNA is damaged, acts as an "emergency brake" to halt the resulting cycle of cell division that can lead to tumor growth and cancer. It also acts as an executioner, programming damaged cells to self-destruct before their altered DNA can be replicated. However, when it mutates, *p53* can lose its suppressive powers or have the devestating effect of actually promoting abnormal cell growth. Indeed, *p53* is the most commonly mutated gene found in human tumors. Currently, researchers are studying exactly how *p53* works and how its properties can be harnessed to treat cancer.

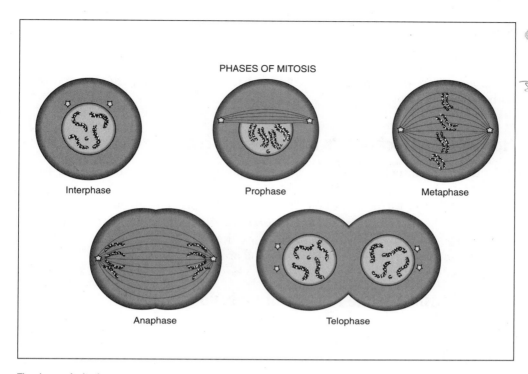

The phases of mitosis.

What are the stages in the type of cell division called **mitosis**?

Cell division in eukaryotes (higher organisms) consists of two stages: *mitosis*, the division of the nucleus, and *cytokinesis*, the division of the whole cell.

The first process in the actual division of the cell is mitosis. In mitosis, the replicated chromosomes are maneuvered so that each new cell gets a full complement of chromosomes—one of each. The process is divided into four phases: prophase, metaphase, anaphase, and telophase.

Nuclear division of sex cells is called meiosis. Sexual reproduction generally requires two parents and it always involves two events (meiosis and fertilization).

Do all cells have a **nucleus**?

Red blood cells are the only cells in the human body that do not have a nucleus. As a result, they cannot divide and so are are produced in bone marrow at the rate of 140,000 per minute. They exist in the body's circulatory system for about 120 days before being destroyed in the liver.

Which organism has the largest number of chromosomes?

Ophioglossum reticulatum, a species of fern, has the largest number of chromosomes with more than 1,260 (630 pairs).

How many **mitochondria** are there in a cell?

The number of mitochondria varies according to the type of cell, but each cell in the human liver has over 1,000 mitochondria. A mitochondrion (singular form) is a self-replicating double-membraned body found in the cytoplasm of all eukaryotic (having a nucleus) cells. The number of mitochondria per cell varies between one and 10,000, and averages about 200. The mitochondria are the sites for much of the metabolism necessary for the production of ATP, lipids, and protein synthesis.

Who is considered the founder of **embryology**?

Kaspar Friedrich Wolff (1733–1794), a German surgeon, is regarded as the founder of embryology. Wolff produced his revolutionary work *Theoria generationis* in 1759. Until that time it was generally believed that each living organism developed from an exact miniature of the adult within the seed or sperm. Wolff introduced the idea that cells in a plant or animal embryo are initially unspecified (undefined) but later differentiate to produce the separate organs and systems with distinct types of tissues.

What does **"ontogeny recapitulates phylogeny"** mean?

Ontogeny is the course of development of an organism from fertilized egg to adult; phylogeny is the evolutionary history of a group of organisms. So the phrase, originating in 19th century biology, means that as an embryo of an advanced organism grows, it will pass through stages that look very much like the adult phase of less advanced organisms. For example, at one point the human embryo has gills and resembles a tadpole.

LIFE PROCESSES, STRUCTURES, ETC.

What is a **biological clock**?

First recognized by the Chinese in the third century B.C.E., the biological clock is an intrinsic mechanism that controls the rhythm of various metabolic activities of plants

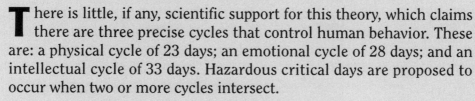

Is there any scientific basis for biorhythms?

There is little, if any, scientific support for this theory, which claims there are three precise cycles that control human behavior. These are: a physical cycle of 23 days; an emotional cycle of 28 days; and an intellectual cycle of 33 days. Hazardous critical days are proposed to occur when two or more cycles intersect.

In contrast, biological rhythms such as activity cycles, feeding cycles, and sleeping cycles, are well-known. They vary from individual to individual and most are tied to the 24 hour rotation period of the Earth. Biological rhythms are real; biorhythms are a hoax.

and animals. Some, such as mating, hibernation, and migration, have a yearly cycle; others, such as ovulation and menstrual cycles of women, follow a lunar month. The majority, however, have a 24-hour, day-night cycle called circadian rhythm. This day-night cycle, first recognized in plants over 250 years ago and existing in virtually all species of plants and animals, regulates these organisms' metabolic functions: plants opening and closing their petals or leaves, germination and flowering functions, changes in human body temperature, hormone secretion, blood sugar and blood pressure levels, and sleep cycles.

Research in chronobiology—the study of these daily rhythms—reveals that many accidents occur between 1 and 6 a.m., that most babies are born in the morning hours, that heart attacks tend to occur between 6 and 9 a.m., and that most Olympic records are broken in the late afternoon. The clock regulator may be the pineal gland located in the heads of animals (including humans).

Who was regarded as the founder of **biochemistry**?

Jan Baptista van Helmont (1577–1644) is called the father of biochemistry because he studied and expressed vital phenomena in chemical terms. The term "biochemistry," coined by F. Hoppe-Seyler in 1877, is the science dealing with the dynamics of living chemical processes or metabolism. It was formed from both the chemists' animal and vegetable chemistry, and the biologists' and doctors' physiological, zoological, or biological chemistry.

Helmont devoted his life to the study of chemistry as the true key to medicine and is considered as one of the founders of modern pathology because he studied the external agents of diseases as well as the anatomical changes caused by diseases.

What is the "Spiegelman monster"?

Sol Spiegelman, an American microbiologist, conducted an experiment to identify the smallest molecule capable of replicating itself. He began with a virus called Q_B, which consisted of a single molecule of ribonucleic acid (RNA) composed of 4,500 nucleotides (units of nucleic acid).

Usually this virus is able to make copies of itself only by invading a living cell because it requires a cellular enzyme called replicase. When Spiegelman added the replicase along with a supply of free nucleotides in a test tube to the virus, the virus replicated itself for several generations when a mutant appeared having fewer than 4,500 nucleotides. Being smaller, this mutant replicated faster than the original virus. Then another mutant appeared and displaced the first, and so it went. Finally, the virus degenerated into a little piece of ribonucleic acid with only 220 nucleotides, the smallest bit necessary for recognizing the replicase. This little test tube monster could continue to replicate at high speed, provided it had a source of building blocks.

Who is **Melvin Calvin**?

Calvin (b. 1911) is an American chemist who won the 1961 Nobel Prize for chemistry for his achievement of working out the chemical reaction cycles called biosynthetic pathways in photosynthesis. Photosynthesis is the process by which green plants use the energy of the sunlight to convert water and carbon dioxide into carbohydrates and oxygen. This cycle of reactions is now called the Calvin cycle. He also conducted research in organometallic chemistry, the chemical origin of life, and taught chemistry at the University of California at Berkeley.

Melvin Calvin.

In addition, Calvin pursued his interest in some unusual applications of chemistry, such as researching oil-bearing plants for their possible development as an alternative energy source. He also was interested in the search for other forms of life that may exist in the universe. During World War II, he developed a process for obtaining pure oxygen directly from the atmosphere. This process has been adapted for a number of applications, such as in machines that provide a continuous supply of oxygen for patients with breathing problems.

CLASSIFICATION, MEASUREMENTS, AND TERMS

What is **radiocarbon dating**?

Radiocarbon dating is a process for determining the age of a prehistoric object by measuring its radiocarbon content. The technique was developed by an American chemist, Dr. Willard F. Libby (1908–1980), in the late 1940s. All living things contain radiocarbon (carbon 14), an isotope that occurs in a small percentage of atmospheric carbon dioxide as a result of cosmic ray bombardment. After an animal or plant dies, it no longer absorbs radiocarbon and the radiocarbon present begins to decay (break down by releasing particles) at an exact and uniform rate. Its half-life of 5,730 years made it useful for measuring prehistory and events occurring within the past 35,000 to 50,000 years. A recent development, called the Accelerated Mass Spectrometer, which separates and detects atomic particles of different mass, can establish more accurate dates with a smaller sample. The remaining radiocarbon can be measured and compared to that of a living sample. In this way, the age of the 50,000 year old or less animal or plant (or more precisely the elapsed time since its death) can be determined.

Since Libby's work, other isotopes having longer half-lives have been used as "geologic clocks" to date very old rocks. The isotope uranium-238 (decaying to lead-206) has a half-life of 4.5 billion years, uranium-235 (decaying to lead-207) has a value of 704 million years, thorium-232 (decaying to lead-278) has a half-life of 14 billion years, rubidium-87 (decaying to strontium-87) has a half-life value of 48.8 billion years, potassium-40 (decaying to argon-40) has a value of 1.25 billion years and samarium-147 (decaying to neodymium-143) has a value of 106 billion years. These isotopes are used in dating techniques of gas formation light emission (called thermoluminescence). Other ways to date the past is dating by tree rings (counting its annual growth rings), and dating by thermoremanent magnetism (the magnetic field of the rock is compared to a date chart of changes in the Earth's magnetic field).

Who coined the term **biology**?

Biology was first used by Karl Burdach (1776–1847) to denote the study of man. Jean Baptiste Pierre Antoine de Monet Lamarck (1744–1829) gave the term a broader meaning in 1812. He believed in the integral character of science. For the special sciences, **149** chemistry, meteorology, geology, and botany-zoology, he coined the term "biology."

Lamarckism epitomizes the belief that changes acquired during an individual's lifetime as the result of active, quasi-purposive, functional adaptations can somehow be imprinted upon the genes, thereby becoming part of the heritage of succeeding generations. Today, very few professional biologists believe that anything of the kind occurs—or can occur.

Biology is the science that deals with living things (Greek *bios*, "life"). Formerly broadly divided into two areas, zoology (Greek *zoon*, "animal"), the study of animals, and botany (Greek *botanes*, "plant"), the study of plants, biology is now divided and sub-divided into hundreds of special fields involving the structure, function, and classification of the forms of life. These include anatomy, ecology, embryology, evolution, genetics, paleontology, and physiology.

Jean Baptiste Pierre Antoine de Monet Lamarck.

Where did the term **molecular biology** originate?

Warren Weaver, the director of the Rockefeller Foundation's Division of Natural Sciences originated the term molecular biology. Weaver used x-ray diffraction to investigate the molecular basis of inheritance and the structure of biological macromolecules. He called this relatively new field molecular biology in a 1938 report.

What is **gnotobiotics**?

Gnotobiotics is the scientific study of animals or other organisms that are raised in germ-free environments or ones that contain only specifically known germs. These animals are first removed from the womb and then are placed in sterilized cages called isolators. Scientists are able to use these animals to determine how specific agents, such as viruses, bacteria, and fungi, affect the body.

What are the **five kingdoms** presently used to categorize living things?

Carolus Linnaeus (1707–1778) in 1735 divided all living things into two kingdoms in his classification system that was based on similarities and differences of organisms.

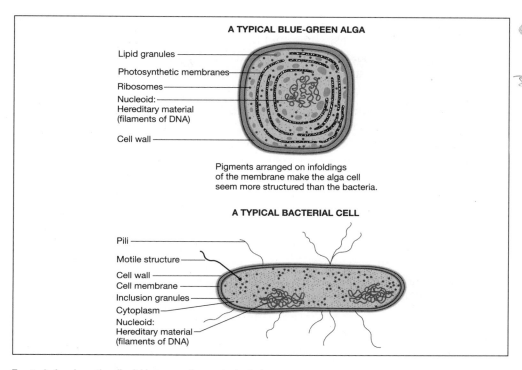

A TYPICAL BLUE-GREEN ALGA

Lipid granules

Photosynthetic membranes

Ribosomes

Nucleoid:
Hereditary material
(filaments of DNA)

Cell wall

Pigments arranged on infoldings
of the membrane make the alga cell
seem more structured than the bacteria.

A TYPICAL BACTERIAL CELL

Pili

Motile structure

Cell wall

Cell membrane

Inclusion granules

Cytoplasm

Nucleoid:
Hereditary material
(filaments of DNA)

Two typical prokaryotic cells: A blue-green algae and a bacteria.

However, since then, fungi seemed not to fit nicely into either kingdom. Although fungi were generally considered plants, they had no chlorophyll, roots, stems, or leaves, and hardly resemble any true plant. They also have several features found in the animal kingdom, as well as unique features characteristic of themselves alone. So fungi was considered the third kingdom. In 1959, R. H. Whittaker proposed the current five kingdom system, based on new evidence from biochemical techniques and electron microscope observations that revealed fundamental differences among organisms. Each kingdom is listed below.

Monera—One-celled organisms lacking a membrane around the cell's genetic matter. Prokaryote (or procaryote) is the term used for this condition where the genetic material lies free in the cytoplasm of the cell without a membrane to form the nucleus of the cell. The kingdom consists of bacteria and blue-green algae (also called blue-green bacteria or cyanobacteria). Bacteria do not produce their own food but blue-green algae do. Blue-green algae, the primary form of life 3.5 to 1.5 billion years ago, produce most of the world's oxygen through photosynthesis.

Protista—Mostly single-celled organisms with a membrane around the cell's genetic material called eukaryotes (or eucaryotes) because of the nuclear mem-

151

brane and other organelles found in the cytoplasm of the cell. Protista consists of true algae, diatoms, slime molds, protozoa, and euglena. Protistans are diverse in their modes of nutrition, etc. They may be living examples of the kinds of ancient single cells that gave rise to the kingdoms of multicelled eukaryotes (fungi, plants, and animals).

Fungi—One-celled or multicelled eukaryotes (having a nuclear membrane or a membrane around the genetic material). The nuclei stream between cells giving the appearance that cells have multiple nuclei. This unique cellular structure, along with the unique sexual reproduction pattern, distinguish the fungi from all other organisms. Consisting of mushrooms, yeasts, molds, etc., the fungi do not produce their own food.

Plantae—Multicellular organisms having cell nuclei and cell walls, which directly or indirectly nourish all other forms of life. Most use photosynthesis (a process by which green plants, containing chlorophyll, utilize sunlight as an energy source to synthesize complex organic material, especially carbohydrates from carbon dioxide, water, and inorganic salts) and most are autotrophs (produce their own food from inorganic matter).

Animalia—Multicellular organisms whose eukaryotic cells (without cell walls) form tissues (and from tissues form organs). Most get their food by ingestion of other organisms; they are heterotrophs (cannot produce their food from inorganic elements). Most are able to move from place to place (mobile) at least during part of the life cycle.

Who devised the current **animal and plant classification** system?

The naming and organizing of the millions of species of plants and animals is frequently called taxonomy; such classifications provide a basis for comparisons and generalizations. A common classification format is an hierarchical arrangement in which a group is classified within a group, and the level of the group is denoted in a ranking.

Carolus Linnaeus (1707–1778) composed a hierarchical classification system for plants (1753) and animals (1758) using a system of nomenclature (naming) that continues to be used today. Every plant and animal was given two scientific

Carolus Linnaeus.

152 names (binomial method) in Latin, one

for the species and the other for the group or genus within the species. He categorized the organisms by perceived physical differences and similarities. Although Linnaeus started with only two kingdoms, contemporary classifiers have expanded them into five kingdoms. Each kingdom is divided into two or more phyla (major groupings; phylum is the singular form). Members within one phylum are more closely related to one another than they are to members of another phylum. These phyla are subdivided into parts again and again; members of each descending level have a closer relationship to each other than those of the level above. Generally the ranking of the system, going from general to specific, are Kingdom, Phylum (plant world uses the term, division), Class, Order, Family, Genus, and Species. In addition, intermediate taxonomic levels can be created by adding the prefixes "sub" or "super" to the name of the level, for example, "subphylum" or "superfamily." Zoologists working on parts of the animal classification, many times are not uniform in their groupings. The system is still evolving and changing as new information emerges and new interpretations develop. Below is listed a comparison of hierarchy for four of the five kingdoms.

Taxonomic level	Human	Grasshopper	White Pine	Typhoid Bacterium
Kingdom	Animalia	Animalia	Plantae	Protista
Phylum	Chordata	Anthropoda	Tracheophyta	Schizomycophyta
Class	Mammalia	Insecta	Gymnospermae	Schizomycetes
Order	Primates	Orthoptera	Coniferales	Eubacteriales
Family	Hominidae	Arcridiidae	Pinaceae	Bacteriaceae
Genus	*Homo*	*Schistocerca*	*Pinus*	*Eberthella*
Species	*sapiens*	*americana*	*strobus*	*typhosa*

How many **different organisms** have been identified by biologists?

Almost 1.5 million different species of plants, animals, and microorganisms are currently known.

FUNGI, BACTERIA, ALGAE, ETC.

What are **diatoms**?

Diatoms are microscopic algae in the phylum *bacillarrophyte* of the protista kingdom. Yellow or brown in color, almost all diatoms are single-celled algae, dwelling in fresh and salt water, especially in the cold waters of the North Pacific Ocean and the Antarc-

> ## How is a fairy ring formed?
>
> A fairy ring, or fungus ring, is found frequently in a grassy area. There are three types: those that do not affect the surrounding vegetation, those that cause increased growth, and those that damage the surrounding environment. The ring is started from a mycelium (the underground, food-absorbing part of a fungus). The fungus growth is on the outer edge of the grassy area because the inner band of decaying mycelium "use-up" the resources in the soil at the center. This creates a ring effect. Each succeeding generation is farther out from the center.

tic. Diatoms are an important food source for marine plankton (floating animal and plant life) and many small animals.

Diatoms have hard cell walls; these "shells" are made from silica that they extract from the water. It is unclear how they accomplish this. When they die, their glassy shells, called frustules, sink to the bottom of the sea, which hardens into rock called diatomite. One of the most famous and accessible diatomites is the Monterrey Formation along the coast of central and southern California.

What is the scientific study of **fungi** called?

Mycology is the science concerning fungi. In the past, fungi have been classified in other kingdoms, but currently they are recognized as a separate kingdom based on their unique cellular structure and their unique pattern of sexual reproduction.

Fungi are heterotrophs (cannot produce their own food from inorganic matter). They secrete enzymes that digest food outside their bodies and their fungal cells absorb the products. Their activities are essential in the decomposition of organic material and cycling of nutrients in nature.

Some fungi, called saprobes, obtain nutrients from non-living organic matter. Other fungi are parasites; they obtain nutrients from the tissues of living host organisms. The great majority of fungi are multicelled and filamentous. A mushroom is a modified reproductive structure in or upon which spores develop. Each spore dispersed from it may grow into a new mushroom.

What is a **lichen**?

Lichens are organisms that grow on rocks, tree branches, or bare ground. They are composed of a green algae and a colorless fungus living together symbiotically. They do not have roots, stems, flowers, or leaves. The fungus, having no chlorophyll, cannot manufacture its own food, but can absorb food from the algae that it enwraps completely, providing protection from the sun and moisture.

This relationship between the fungus and algae is called symbiosis (a close association of two organisms not necessarily to both their benefits). Lichens were the first recognized and are still the best examples of this phenomenon. An unique feature of lichen symbiosis is that it is so perfectly developed and balanced as to behave as a single organism.

Are there **stone-eating bacteria**?

Stone-eating bacteria belong to several families in the genus *Thiobacillus*. They can cause damage to monuments, tombs, buildings, and sculptures by converting marble into plaster. The principal danger seems to come from *Thiobacillus thioparus*. This microbe's metabolic system converts sulfur dioxide gas (found in the air) into sulfuric acid and uses it to transform calcium carbonate (marble) into calcium sulfate (plaster). The bacilli draw their nutrition from carbon dioxide formed in the transformation.

Nitrobacter and *Nitrosomonas* are other "stone-eating bacteria" that use ammonia from the air to generate nitric and nitrous acid. Still other kinds of bacteria and fungi can produce organic acids (formic, acetic, and oxalic acids) that attack the stone as well. The presence of these microbes was first observed by a French scientist, Henri Pochon at Angkor Wat, Cambodia, during the 1950s. The increase of these bacteria and other biological-damaging organisms that threaten tombs and buildings of antiquity are due to the sharp climb in the level of free sulfur dioxide gas in the atmosphere from automotive and industrial emissions.

Who was first to coin the word **virus**?

The English physician Edward Jenner (1749–1823), founder of virology and a pioneer in vaccination, first coined the word "virus". Using one virus to immunize against another one was precisely the strategy Jenner used when he inoculated someone with cowpox (a disease that attacks cows) to make them immune to smallpox. This procedure is called vaccination from *vaccine* (the Latin name for cowpox). Vaccines are usually a very mild dose of the disease-causing bacteria or virus (weakened or dead). These vaccines stimulate the creation of antibodies in the body that recognize and attack a particular infection. A virus is a minute parasitic organism that reproduces only inside the cell of its host. Viruses replicate by invading host cells and taking over the cell's "machinery" for DNA replication. Viral particles then can break out of the cells, causing disease.

Who were the founders of **modern bacteriology**?

The German bacteriologist, Robert Koch (1843–1910), and the French chemist, Louis Pasteur (1822–1895), are considered the founders. Pasteur devised a way to heat food or beverages at a temperature slow enough not to ruin them, but high enough to kill **155** most of the microorganisms that would cause spoilage and disease. This process is called pasteurization. By demonstrating that tuberculosis was an infectious disease caused by a specific *bacillus* and not by bad heredity, Koch laid the groundwork for public health measures that would significantly reduce such diseases. His working methodologies for isolating microorganisms, his laboratory procedures, and his four postulates for determination of disease agents gave medical investigators valuable insights into the control of bacterial infections.

Why are **Koch's postulates** significant?

The German bacteriologist, Robert Koch (1843–1910), developed four rules in his study of disease-producing organisms, which later investigators found useful. The following conditions must be met to prove that a bacterium causes a particular disease:

1. The microorganism must be found in large numbers in all diseased animals but not in healthy ones.
2. The organism must be isolated from a diseased animal and grown outside the body in a pure culture.
3. When the isolated microorganism is injected into other healthy animals, it must produce the same disease.
4. The suspected microorganism must be recovered from the experimental hosts, isolated, compared to the first microorganism, and found to be identical.

COMMUNICATIONS

SYMBOLS, WRITING, AND CODES

Which **animals** other than horses have been used to **deliver the mail**?

During the 19th century, cows hauled mail wagons in some German towns. In Texas, New Mexico, and Arizona, camels were used. In Russia and Scandinavia, reindeer pulled mail sleighs. The Belgian city of Liége even tried cats, but they proved to be unreliable.

What is the **standard phonetic alphabet**?

Letter	Phonetic equivalent
A	Alpha
B	Bravo
C	Charlie
D	Delta
E	Echo
F	Fox Trot
G	Golf
H	Hotel
I	India
J	Juliett
K	Kilo
L	Lima

Letter	Phonetic equivalent
M	Mike
N	November
O	Oscar
P	Papa
Q	Quebec
R	Romeo
S	Sierra
T	Tango
U	Uniform
V	Victor
W	Whiskey
X	X-ray
Y	Yankee
Z	Zulu

Who invented the **Braille** alphabet?

The Braille system, used by the blind to read and write, consists of combinations of raised dots that form characters corresponding to the letters of the alphabet, punctuation marks, and common words such as "and" and "the." Louis Braille (1809–1852), blind himself since the age of three, began working on developing a practical alphabet for the blind shortly after he started a school for the blind in Paris. He experimented with a communication method called night-writing, which the French army used for nighttime battlefield missives. With the assistance of an army officer, Captain Charles Barbier, Braille pared the method's 12-dot configurations to a 6-dot one and devised a code of 63 characters. The system was not widely accepted for several years; even Braille's own Paris school did not adopt the system until 1854, two years after his death. In 1916, the United States sanctioned Louis Braille's original system of raised dots, and in 1932 a modification called "Standard English Braille, Grade 2" was adopted throughout the English-speaking world. The revised version changed the letter-by-letter codes into common letter combinations, such as "ow," "ing," and "ment," making reading and writing a faster activity.

Before Braille's system, one of the few effective alphabets for the blind was devised by another Frenchman, Valentin Haüy (1745–1822), who was the first to emboss paper to help the blind read. Haüy's letters in relief were actually a punched alphabet, and imitators immediately began to copy and improve on his system. Another letter-by-letter system of nine basic characters was devised by Dr. William Moon (1818–1894) in 1847, but it is less versatile in its applications.

What is the **Morse Code**?

The success of any electrical communication system lies in its coding interpretation,

What is a hornbook?

Found in English and American classrooms from the 15th century to the 18th century, the hornbook was a flat board with a handle that beginning students used. On the board was pasted a sheet of paper usually containing the alphabet, the Benediction, the Lord's Prayer, and the Roman numerals. A thin, flat piece of clear horn covered the whole board to protect the paper, which was scarce and expensive at the time. Hornbooks were used as early as 1442 and became standard equipment in English schools by the 1500s. They were discontinued around 1800, when books became cheaper.

Samuel F. B. Morse.

for only series of electric impulses can be transmitted from one end of the system to the other. These impulses must be "translated" from and into words, numbers, etc. This problem plagued early telegraphy until American painter-turned-scientist Samuel F. B. Morse (1791–1872), with the help of Alfred Vail (1807–1859), devised in 1835 a code composed of dots and dashes to represent letters, numbers, and punctuation. Telegraphy uses an electromagnet—a device that becomes magnetic when activated and raps against a metal contact. A series of short electrical impulses repeatedly can make and break this magnetism, resulting in a tapped-out message.

Having secured a patent on the code in 1837, Morse and Vail established a communications company on May 24, 1844. The first long-distance telegraphed message was sent by Morse in Washington, D.C., to Vail in Baltimore, Maryland. This was the same year that Morse took out a patent on telegraphy; Morse never acknowledged the unpatented contributions of Joseph Henry (1797–1878), who invented the first electric motor and working electromagnet in 1829 and the electric telegraph in 1831.

The International Morse Code (shown below) uses sound or a flashing light to send messages. The dot is a very short sound or flash; a dash equals three dots. The pauses between sounds or flashes should equal one dot. An interval of the length of one dash is left between letters; an interval of two dashes is left between words.

A .-	J .—	S ...
B -...	K -.-	T -
C -.-.	L .-..	U ..—
D -..	M —	V ...-
E .	N -.	W .—
F ..-.	O —	X -..-
G —.	P .—.	Y -.—
H	Q —.-	Z —..
I ..	R .-.	
1 .——	6 -....	Period .-.-.-
2 ..——	7 —...	Comma —..—
3 ...—	8 —..	
4 ....-	9 —.	
5	0 ———	

What were **Enigma** and **Purple** in **World War II**?

Enigma and *Purple* were the electric rotor cipher machines of the Germans and Japanese, respectively. The Enigma machine, used by the Nazis, was invented in the 1920s and was the best known cipher machine in history. One of the greatest triumphs in the history of cryptanalysis was the Polish and British solution of the German Enigma ciphers. This played a major role in the Allies' conduct of World War II.

In 1939, the Japanese introduced a new cipher machine adapted from *Enigma*. Code-named *Purple* by U.S. cryptanalysts, the new machine used telephone stepping switches instead of rotors. U.S. cryptanalysts were able to solve this new system as well.

Cryptography—the art of sending messages in such a way that the real meaning is hidden from everyone but the sender and the recipient—is done in two ways: code and cipher. A code is like a dictionary in which all the words and phrases are replaced by codewords or codenumbers. A codebook is used to read the code. A cipher works with single letters, rather than complete words or phrases. There are two kinds of ciphers: transposition and substitution. In a transposition cipher, the letters of the ordinary message (or plain text) are jumbled to form the cipher text. In substitution, the plain letters can be replaced by other letters, numbers, or symbols.

What are the **10-codes**?

Almost as many different codes exist as agencies using codes in radio transmission. The following are officially suggested by the Associated Public Safety Communications

Officers (APSCO):

Ten-1   Cannot understand your message.
Ten-2   Your signal is good.
Ten-3   Stop transmitting.
Ten-4   Message received ("O.K.").
Ten-5   Relay information to _____.
Ten-6   Station is busy.
Ten-7   Out of service.
Ten-8   In service.
Ten-9   Repeat last message.
Ten-10   Negative ("no").
Ten-11   _____ in service.
Ten-12   Stand by.
Ten-13   Report _____ conditions.
Ten-14   Information.
Ten-15   Message delivered.
Ten-16   Reply to message.
Ten-17   Enroute.
Ten-18   Urgent.
Ten-19   Contact _____.
Ten-20   Unit location.
Ten-21   Call _____ by telephone.
Ten-22   Cancel last message.
Ten-23   Arrived at scene.
Ten-24   Assignment completed.
Ten-25   Meet _____.
Ten-26   Estimated time of arrival is _____.
Ten-27   Request for information on license.
Ten-28   Request vehicle registration information.
Ten-29   Check records.
Ten-30   Use caution.
Ten-31   Pick up.
Ten-32   Units requested.
Ten-33   Emergency! Officer needs help.
Ten-34   Correct time.

What do the lines in a UPC bar code mean?

A Universal Product Code (UPC) or bar code is a product description code designed to be read by a computerized scanner or cash register. It consists of 11 numbers in groups of "0"s (dark strips) and "1"s (white strips). A bar will be thin if it has only one strip or thicker if there are two or more strips side by side.

The first number describes the type of product. Most products begin with a "0"; exceptions are variable weight products such as meat and vegetables (2), health-care products (3), bulk-discounted goods (4), and coupons (5). Since it might be misread as a bar, the number 1 is not used.

The next five numbers describe the product's manufacturer. The five numbers after that describe the product itself, including its color, weight, size, and other distinguishing characteristics. The code does not include the price of the item. When the identifying code is read, the information is sent to the store's computer database, which checks it against a price list and returns the price to the cash register.

The last number is a check digit, which tells the scanner if there is an error in the other numbers. The preceding numbers, when added, multiplied, and subtracted in a certain way will equal this number. If they do not, a mistake exists somewhere.

What does the code that follows the letters ISBN mean?

ISBN, or International Standard Book Number, is an ordering and identifying code for book products. It forms a unique number to identify that particular item. The first number of the series relates to the language the book is published in, for example, the zero is designated for the English language. The second set of numbers identifies the publisher, and the last set of numbers identifies the particular item. The very last number is a "check number," which mathematically makes certain that the previous numbers have been entered correctly.

RADIO AND TELEVISION

Who invented radio?

Guglielmo Marconi (1874–1937), of Bologna, Italy, was the first to prove that radio signals could be sent over long distances. Radio is the radiation and detection of signals propagated through space as electromagnetic waves to convey information. It was first called wireless telegraphy because it duplicated the effect of telegraphy without using wires. On December 12, 1901, Marconi successfully sent Morse code signals from Newfoundland to England.

In 1906, the American inventor Lee de Forest (1873–1961) built what he called "the Audion," which became the basis for the radio amplifying vacuum tube. This device made voice radio practical, because it magnified the weak signals without distorting them. The next year, de Forest began regular radio broadcasts from Manhattan, New York. As there were still no home radio receivers, de Forest's only audience was ship wireless operators in New York City Harbor.

What was the first **radio broadcasting station**?

The identity of the "first" broadcasting station is a matter of debate since some pioneer AM broadcast stations developed from experimental operations begun before the institution of formal licensing practices. According to records of the Department of Commerce, which then supervised radio, WBZ in Springfield, Massachusetts, received the first regular broadcasting license on September 15, 1921. However, credit for the first radio broadcasting station has customarily gone to Westinghouse station KDKA in Pittsburgh for its broadcast of the Harding-Cox presidential election returns on November 2, 1920. Unlike most other earlier radio transmissions, KDKA used electron tube technology to generate the transmitted signal and hence to have what could be described as broadcast quality. It was the first corporate-sponsored radio station and the first

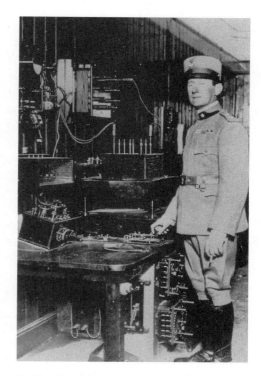

Guglielmo Marconi with his wireless radio.

to have a well-defined commercial purpose—it was not a hobby or a publicity stunt. It was the first broadcast station to be licensed on a frequency outside the amateur bands. Altogether, it was the direct ancestor of modern broadcasting.

How are the **call letters** beginning with "K" or "W" assigned to **radio stations**?

These beginning call letters are assigned on a geographical basis. For the majority of radio stations located east of the Mississippi River, their call letters begin with the letter "W"; if the stations are west of the Mississippi, their first call letter is the letter "K". There are exceptions to this rule. Stations founded before this rule went into effect kept their old letters. So, for example, KDKA in Pittsburgh has retained the first letter "K"; likewise some western pioneer stations have retained the letter "W". Since many **163**

AM licensees also operate FM and TV stations, a common practice is to use the AM call letters followed by "–FM" or "–TV".

Why do **FM radio stations** have a limited broadcast range?

Usually radio waves higher in frequency than approximately 50 to 60 megahertz are not reflected by the Earth's ionosphere, but are lost in space. Television, FM radio, and high frequency communications systems are therefore limited to approximately line-of0sight ranges. The line-of-sight distance depends on the terrain and antenna height, but is usually limited to from 50 to 100 miles (80 to 161 kilometers). FM (frequency–modulation) radio uses a wider band than AM (amplitude–modulation) radio to give broadcasts high fidelity, especially noticeable in music—crystal clarity to high frequencies and rich resonance to base notes, all with a minimum of static and distortion. Invented by Edwin Howard Armstrong (1891–1954) in 1933, FM receivers became available in 1939.

Edwin Howard Armstrong.

Why do **AM stations** have a wider **broadcast range at night**?

This variation is caused by the nature of the ionosphere of the Earth. The ionosphere consists of several different layers of rarefied gases in the upper atmosphere that have become conductive through the bombardment of the atoms of the atmosphere by solar radiation, by electrons and protons emitted by the sun, and by cosmic rays. These layers, sometimes called the Kennelly–Heaviside layer, reflect AM radio signals, enabling AM broadcasts to be received by radios that are great distances from the transmitting antenna. With the coming of night, the ionosphere layers partially dissipate and become an excellent reflector of the short waveband AM radio waves. This causes distant AM stations to be heard more clearly at night.

Can **radio transmissions** between **space shuttles** and ground control be picked up by shortwave radio?

Amateur radio operators at Goddard Space Flight Center, Greenbelt, Maryland, retransmit shuttle space-to-ground radio conversations on shortwave frequencies. These retransmissions can be heard freely around the world. To hear astronauts talking with ground controllers during liftoff, flight, and landing, a shortwave radio capable of receiving single-sideband signals should be tuned to frequencies of 3.860, 7.185, 14.295, and 21.395 megahertz. British physics teacher Geoffrey Perry, at the Kettering Boys School, has taught his students how to obtain telemetry from orbiting Russian satellites. Since the early 1960s Perry's students have been monitoring Russian space signals using a simple taxicab radio, and using the data to calculate position and orbits of the spacecraft.

Who was the founder of **television**?

The idea of television (or "seeing by electricity," as it was called in 1880) was offered by several people over the years, and several individuals contributed a multiplicity of partial inventions. For example, in 1897 Ferdinand Braun (1850–1918) constructed the first cathode ray oscilloscope, a fundamental component to all television receivers. In 1907, Boris Rosing proposed using Braun's tube to receive images, and in the following year Alan Campbell-Swinton likewise suggested using the tube, now called the cathode-ray tube, for both transmission and receiving. The figure most frequently called the father of television, however, was a Russian-born American named Vladimir K. Zworykin (1889–1982). A former pupil of Rosing, he produced a practical method of amplifying the electron beam so that the light/dark pattern would produce a good image. In 1923, he patented the iconoscope (which would become the television camera), and in 1924 he patented the kinoscope (television tube). Both inventions rely on streams of electrons for both scanning and creating the image on a fluorescent screen. By 1938, after adding new and more sensitive photo cells, Zworykin demonstrated his first practical model.

Another "father" of television is the American Philo T. Farnsworth. He was the first person to propose that pictures could be televised electronically. He came up with the basic design for an apparatus in 1922 and discussed his ideas with his high school teacher. This documented his ideas one year before Zworykin and was critical in settling a patent dispute between Farnsworth and his competitor at the Radio Corporation of America. Farnsworth eventually licensed his television patents to the growing industry and let others refine and develop his basic inventions.

During the early 20th century others worked on different approaches to television. The best-known is John Logie Baird (1888–1946), who in 1936 used a mechanized scanning device to transmit the first recognizable picture of a human face. Limitations in his designs made any further improvements in the picture quality impossible.

How does **rain** affect **television reception** from a satellite?

The incoming microwave signals are absorbed by rain and moisture, and severe rainstorms can reduce signals by as much as 10 decibels (reduction by a factor of 10). If **165** the installation cannot cope with this level of signal reduction, the picture may be momentarily lost. Even quite moderate rainfall can reduce signals enough to give noisy reception on some receivers. Another problem associated with rain is an increase in noise due to its inherent noise temperature. Any body above the temperature of absolute zero (0°K or -459°F or -273°C) has an inherent noise temperature generated by the release of wave packets from the body's molecular agitation (heat). These wave packets have a wide range of frequencies, some of which will be within the required bandwidth for satellite reception. The warm Earth has a high noise temperature, and consequently rain does as well.

What name is used for a **satellite dish** that picks up **TV broadcasts**?

Earth station is the term used for the complete satellite receiving or transmitting station. It includes the antenna, the electronics, and all associated equipment necessary to receive or transmit satellite signals. It can range from a simple, inexpensive, receive-only Earth station that can be purchased by the individual consumer, to elaborate, two-way communications stations that offer commercial access to the satellite's capacity. Signals are captured and focused by the antenna into a feedhorn and low noise amplifier. These are relayed by cable to a down converter and then into the satellite receiver/modulator.

Satellite television became widely available in the late 1970s when cable television stations, equipped with satellite dishes, received signals and sent them to their subscribers by coaxial cable. Taylor Howard designed the first satellite dish for personal use in 1976. By 1984 there were 500,000 installations, and in recent years that number has increased worldwide to 3.7 million.

What is **high definition television**?

The amount of detail shown in a television picture is limited by the number of lines that make it up and by the number of picture elements on each line. The latter is mostly determined by the width of the electron beam. To obtain pictures closer to the quality associated with 35-millimeter photography, a new television system, HDTV (High Definition Television) will have more than twice the number of scan lines with a much smaller picture element. Currently American and Japanese television has 525 scanning lines, while Europe uses 625 scanning lines. HDTV has received wide publicity in recent years, but it is currently in an engineering phase, and not yet commercially available.

The Japanese are generally given credit for being pioneers in HDTV, ever since the Japanese broadcasting company NHK began research in 1968. In fact, the original pioneer was RCA's Otto Schade who began his research after the end of World War II.

Can a TV satellite dish be painted a different color?

Although not recommended, TV satellite dishes can be painted a different color as long as the same standards adhered to in manufacture are maintained. The paint used should not be optically reflective. Metallic paints or gloss finishes may focus the sun's radiation on the head unit, causing performance problems. Only "vinyl matte" finish paints should be used. They exhibit lower solar reflection properties, and they cause a minimal amount of microwave absorption and reflection errors. Finally, the paint should be applied as smoothly as possible, as any bumps or drips may cause reflection errors.

Schade was ahead of his time, and decades passed before television pickup tubes and other components became available to take full advantage of his research.

HDTV cannot be used in the commercial broadcast bands until technical standards are approved by the United States Federal Communications Commission (FCC) or the various foreign regulating agencies. The more immediate problem, however, has been a technological one—HDTV needs to transmit five times more data than is currently assigned to each television channel. One approach is signal compression—squeezing the 30-megahertz bandwidth signal that HDTV requires into the six-megahertz bandwidth currently used for television broadcasting. The Japanese and Europeans have explored analog systems that use wavelike transmission, while the Americans based their HDTV development on digital transmission systems. In 1994, the television industry cleared this hurdle when it accepted a digital signal transmission system developed by Zenith. However, HDTV sets won't be available to the public until 1997 or later, and at prices ranging from $3,500 to $5,000.

How do submerged **submarines communicate**?

Using frequencies from very high to extremely low, submarines can communicate by radio when submerged if certain conditions are met, and depending on whether or not detection is important. Submarines seldom transmit on long-range high radio frequencies if detection is important, as in war. However, Super (SHF), Ultra (UHF), or Very High Frequency (VHF) two-way links with cooperating aircraft, surface ships, via satellite, or with the shore are fairly safe with high data rate, though they all require that the boat show an antenna or send a buoy to the surface.

TELECOMMUNICATIONS, RECORDINGS, THE INTERNET, ETC.

When was the first **commercial communications satellite** used?

In 1960 *ECHO 1*, the first communications satellite, was launched. Two years later, on July 10, 1962, the first commercially funded satellite, *Telstar 1* (paid for by American Telephone and Telegraph), was launched into low Earth orbit. It was also the first true communications satellite, being able to relay not only data and voice, but television as well. The first broadcast, which was relayed from the United States to England, showed an American flag flapping in the breeze. The first commercial satellite (in which its operations are conducted like a business) was *Early Bird*, which went into regular service on June 10, 1965, with 240 telephone circuits. *Early Bird* was the first satellite launched for Intelsat (International Telecommunications Satellite Organization). Still in existence, the system is owned by member nations—each nation's contribution to the operating funds are based on its share of the system's annual traffic.

How does a **fax machine** work?

Telefacsimile (also telefax or facsimile or fax) transmits graphic and textual information from one location to another through telephone lines. A transmitting machine uses either a digital or analog scanner to convert the black and white representations of the image into electrical signals that are transmitted through the telephone lines to a designated receiving machine. The receiving unit converts the transmission back to an image of the original and prints it. In its broadest definition, a facsimile terminal is simply a copier equipped to transmit and receive graphics images.

The fax was invented by Alexander Bain of Scotland in 1842. His crude device, along with scanning systems invented by Frederick Bakewell in 1848, evolved into several modern versions. In 1924, faxes were first used to transmit wire photos from Cleveland to New York, a boon to the newspaper industry.

Can a **fax** and an **answering machine** be used on the same telephone line?

Most fax machines come with an interface that allows it to work with an answering machine. The fax "listens" for the incoming call and sends it to the answering machine if no one picks up the phone. As the message is being recorded, the fax machine listens for a fax tone. If it hears the tone, it sends the fax through. If not, the answering machine continues to function as it normally would. Fax machines with built–in answering machines are also available, making such an interface unnecessary.

What is a **fiber optic cable**?

A fiber optic cable is composed of many very thin strands of coated glass fibers that transmit light through the process of "cladding," in which total internal reflection of light is achieved by using material that has a lower refractive index. Once light enters the fiber, the cladding layer inside it prevents light loss as the beam of light zigzags inside the glass core. Glass fibers can transmit messages or images by directing beams of light inside itself over very short or very long distances up to 13,000 miles (20,917 kilometers) without significant distortion. The pattern of light waves forms a code that carries a message. At the receiving end, the light beams are converted back into electric current and decoded. Since light beams are immune to electrical noise and can be carried greater distances before fading, this technology is used heavily in telecommunications. Other applications include using

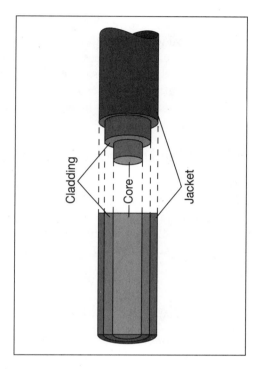

A cross section of a fiber optic cable.

medical fiber optic viewers, such as endoscopes and fiberscopes, to see internal organs; fiber optic message devices in aircraft and space vehicles; and fiber optic connections in automotive lighting systems.

What is a **Clarke belt**?

Back in 1945, Arthur C. Clarke (b. 1917), the famous scientist and science fiction writer, predicted that an artificial satellite placed at a height of 22,248 miles (35,803 kilometers) directly above the equator would orbit the globe at the same speed with which the Earth was rotating. As a result, the satellite would remain stationary with respect to any point on the Earth's surface. This equatorial belt, rather like one of Saturn's rings, is affectionately known as the Clarke belt.

What are the types of **cellular telephones**?

There are three types of cellular phones. The first and oldest variety of mobile cellular **169** phones are permanently attached to an automobile and are powered by the car's battery. They also have an antenna that must be mounted outside the vehicle. The second type are transportable, or bag, cellular phones. These are essentially mobile phones with their own battery packs that allow owners to detach them from the car and carry them in a pouch. However, most weigh about five pounds (2.25 kilograms) and are not very practical when used this way. The third type are portable cellular phones. Similar in appearance to a cordless phone handset, a portable generally weighs less than a pound and is the most versatile type of cellular phone. It is also the most expensive and has a transmitter of less power than a mobile or transportable cellular phone. Kits are available for some models, however, that boosts the transmitter's power.

What is the **Dolby** noise reduction system?

The magnetic action of a tape produces a background hiss—a drawback in sound reproduction on tape. A noise reduction system known as *Dolby*—named after R. M. Dolby (b. 1933), its American inventor—is widely used to deal with the hiss. In quiet passages, electronic circuits automatically boost the signals before they reach the recording head, drowning out the hiss. On playback, the signals are reduced to their correct levels. The hiss is reduced at the same time, becoming inaudible.

What is **digital audio tape** (DAT)?

DAT, a new concept in magnetic recording, produces a mathematical value for each sound based on the binary code. When the values are reconstructed during playback, the reconstructed sound is so much like the original that the human ear cannot distinguish the difference. The reproduction is so good that American record companies have lobbied lawmakers to prevent DAT from being sold in the United States, claiming that it could encourage illegal CD copying.

How are **compact discs** (CDs) made?

The master disc for a CD is an optically flat glass disc coated with a resist. The resist is a chemical that is impervious to an etchant that dissolves glass. The master is placed on a turntable. The digital signal to be recorded is fedto the laser, turning the laser off and on in response to the binary on-off signal. When the laser is on, it burns away a small amount of the resist on the disc. While the disc turns, the recording head moves across the disc, leaving a spiral track of elongated "burns" in the resist surface. After the recording is complete, the glass master is placed in the chemical etchant bath. This developing removes the glass only where the resist is burned away. The spiral track now contains a series of small pits of varying length and constant depth. To play a recorded CD, a laser beam scans the three miles (five kilometers) of playing track and converts the "pits" and "lands" of the CD into binary codes. A pho-

What is virtual reality?

Virtual reality combines state-of-the-art imaging with computer technology to allow users to experience a simulated environment as reality. Several different technologies are integrated into a virtual reality system, including holography, which uses lasers to create three-dimensional images; liquid crystal displays; high definition television; and multimedia techniques that combine various types of displays in a single computer terminal.

Despite the widespread attention the media pays to virtual reality, the field remains in a rudimentary state since supporting technologies have yet to meet human expectations.

todiode converts these into a coded string of electrical impulses. In October 1982, the first CDs were marketed; they were invented by Phillips (Netherlands) Company and Sony in Japan in 1978.

What is the lifespan of a **CD-ROM** disc?

Although manufacturers claim that a CD-ROM disc will last 20 years, recent statements by the United States National Archives and Records Administration suggest that a lifespan of three to five years is more accurate. The main problem is that the aluminum substratum on which the data is recorded is vulnerable to oxidation.

What is the **information highway**?

A term originally coined by Vice President Al Gore, the information highway is envisioned as an electronic communications network of the near future that would easily connect all users to one another and provide any every type of electronic service possible, including shopping, electronic banking, education, medical diagnosis, video conferencing, and game playing. Initially implemented on a national scale, it would eventually become a global network.

The exact form of the information highway is a matter of some debate. Two principle views currently exist. One visualizes the highway as a more elaborate form of the Internet, the principle purpose of which would be to gather and exchange written information via a global electronic mail network. The other possibility centers around **171** plans to create an enhanced interactive television network that would provide video services on demand.

What is the **Internet**?

The Internet is the world's largest computer network. It links computer terminals together via wires or telephone lines in a web of networks and shared software. With the proper equipment, an individual can access vast amounts of information and search databases on various computers connected to the Internet, or communicate with someone located anywhere in the world as long as he or she has the proper equipment. Researchers estimate that 20 to 30 million people accessed this system in mid-1995.

Originally created in the late 1960s by the U.S. Department of Defense Advanced Research Projects Agency to share information with other researchers, the Internet mushroomed when scientists and academics using the network discovered its great value. Despite its origin, however, the Internet is not owned or funded by the U.S. government or any other organization or institution. A group of volunteers, the Internet Society, address such issues as daily operations and techincal standards.

What is the **Netplex**?

The Netplex is the name given to an area around Washington, D.C., that has become the world center of the data communications industry and the focal point of the Internet. The businesses in the Netplex include companies that build and manage optical fiber networks, sell Internet connections to companies and individuals, or offer other services. It has been compared to such other "technology centers" as California's Silicon Valley or the Research Triangle of North Carolina, where a large concentration of corporations involved in the telecommunication and computer industries are located.

COMPUTERS

What is an **algorithm**?

An algorithm is a set of clearly defined rules and instructions for the solution of a problem. It is not necessarily applied only in computers, but can be a step-by-step procedure for solving any particular kind of problem. A nearly 4,000-year-old Babylonian banking calculation inscribed on a tablet is an algorithm, as is a computer program that consists of step-by-step procedures for solving a problem.

The term is derived from the name of Muhammad ibn Musa al Kharizmi (ca. 780–ca. 850), a Baghdad mathematician who introduced Hindu numerals (including

0) and decimal calculation to the West. When his treatise was translated into Latin in the 12th century, the art of computation with Arabic (Hindu) numerals became known as *algorism*.

Who invented the **computer**?

Computers developed from calculating machines. One of the earliest mechanical devices for calculating, still widely used today, is the abacus—a frame carrying parallel rods on which beads or counters are strung. Herodotus, the Greek historian who lived around 400 B.C.E., mentions the use of the abacus in Egypt. In 1617, John Napier (1550–1617) invented "Napier's Bones"—marked pieces of ivory for multiples of numbers. In the middle of the same century, Blaise Pascal (1623–1662) produced a simple mechanism for adding and subtracting. Multiplication by repeated addition was a feature of a stepped drum or wheel machine of 1694 invented by Gottfried Wilhelm Leibniz (1646–1716). In

Charles Babbage.

1823, the English visionary Charles Babbage (1792–1871) persuaded the British government to finance an "analytical engine." This would have been a machine that could undertake any kind of calculation. It would have been driven by steam, but the most important innovation was that the entire program of operations was stored on a punched tape. Babbage's machine was not completed and would not have worked if it had been. The standards required were far beyond the capabilities of the engineers of the time, and in any case, rods, levers, and cogs move too slowly for really quick calculations. Modern computers use electrons, which travel at near the speed of light. Although he never built a working computer, Babbage thought out many of the basic principles that guide modern computers.

Based on the concepts of British mathematician Alan M. Turing (1912–1954), the earliest programmable electronic computer was the 1,500-valve "Colossus," formulated by Max Newman (1897–1985), built by T. H. Flowers, and used by the British government in 1943 to crack the German codes generated by the coding machine "Enigma."

What was the first major use for **punched cards**?

Punched cards were a way of programming, or giving instructions to, a machine. In 1801, Joseph Marie Jacquard (1752–1834) built a device that could do automated pat- **173** tern weaving. Cards with holes were used to direct threads in the loom, creating pre-defined patterns in the cloth. The pattern was determined by the arrangement of holes in the cards, with wire hooks passing through the holes to grab and pull through specific threads to be woven into the cloth.

By the 1880s, Herman Hollerith (1860–1929) was using the idea of punched cards to give machines instructions. He built a punched card tabulator that processed the data gathered for the 1890 United States Census in six weeks (three times the speed of previous compilations). Metal pins in the machine's reader passed through holes punched in cards the size of dollar bills, momentarily closing electric circuits. The resulting pulses advanced counters assigned to details such as income and family size. A sorter could also be programmed to pigeonhole cards according to pattern of holes, an important aid in analyzing census statistics. Later, Hollerith founded Tabulating Machines Co., which in 1924 became IBM. When IBM adopted the 80-column punched card (measuring $7\,^3/_8 \times 3\,^1/_4$ inches [18.7 $\times$ 8.25 centimeters] and 0.007 inches [0.17 millimeters] thick), the de facto industry standard was set, which has endured for decades.

What is meant by **fifth generation computers**? What are the other four generations?

The evolution of computers has advanced so much in the past few decades that "generations" are used to describe these important advances:

First generation computer—a mammoth computer using vacuum tubes, drum memories, and programming in machine code as its basic technology. Univax 1, used in 1951, was one of the earliest of these vacuum-tube based electronic computers. The generation starts at the end of World War II and ends about 1957.

Second generation computer—a computer using discrete transistors as its basic technology. Solid-state components replaced the vacuum tubes during this period from 1958 to 1963. Magnetic core memories store information. This era includes the development of high-level computer languages.

Third generation computer—a computer having integrated circuits, semiconductor memories, and magnetic disk storage. New operating systems, minicomputer systems, virtual memory, and timesharing are the advancements of this period from 1963 to 1971.

Fourth generation computer—a computer using microprocessors and large-scale integrated chips as its basic technology, which made computers accessible to a large segment of the population. Networking, improved memory, database management systems, and advanced languages mark the period from 1971 to the end of the 1980s.

Fifth generation computer—a computer that uses inference to draw reasoned conclusions from a knowledge base, and interacts with its users via an intelligent

What is the origin of the expression "Do not fold, spindle, or mutilate"?

This is the inscription on an IBM punched card. Frequently, office workers organize papers and forms by stapling or folding them together, or by impaling them on a spindle. Because Hollerith (punched) card readers scan uniform rectangular holes in a precise arrangement, any damage to the physical card makes it unusable. In the 1950s and 1960s, when punched cards became widespread, manufacturers printed a warning on each card; IBM's "Do not fold, spindle, or mutilate" was the best known. In 1964, the student revolution at the University of California, Berkeley used the phrase as a symbol of authority and regimentation.

user interface to perform such functions as speech recognition, machine translation of natural languages, and robotic operations. These computers using artificial intelligence have been under development since the early 1980s, especially in Japan, as well as in the United States and Europe. In 1991, however, Japan began a new 10-year initiative to investigate neural networks, which will probably divert resources from development of the fifth generation as traditionally defined.

A lot of people have heard of ENIAC, the first large electronic computer. What was MANIAC?

MANIAC (mathematical analyzer, numerator, integrator, and computer) was built at the Los Alamos Scientific Laboratory under the direction of Nicholas C. Metropolis between 1948 and 1952. It was one of several different copies of the high-speed computer built by John von Neumann (1903–1957) for the Institute for Advanced Studies (IAS). It was constructed primarily for use in the development of atomic energy applications, specifically the hydrogen bomb.

It was originated with the work on ENIAC (electronic numerical integrator and computer), the first fully operational, large-scale, electronic digital computer. ENIAC was built at the Moore School of Electrical Engineering at the University of Pennsylvania between 1943 and 1946. Its builders, John Prosper Eckert Jr. and John William Mauchly (1907–1980), virtually launched the modern era of the computer with ENIAC.

What is an **expert system**?

An expert system is a type of software that analyzes a complex problem in a particular field and recommends possible solutions based on information previously programmed into it. The person who develops an expert system first analyzes the behavior of a human expert in a given field, then inputs all the explicit rules resulting from their study into the system. Expert systems are used in equipment repair, insurance planning, training, medical diagnosis, and other areas.

For what purpose was **MADAM** designed?

MADAM (Manchester automatic digital machine) is a chess-playing machine designed by Alan M. Turing (1912–1954) in 1950. Turing was one of the first individuals to program a computer to play chess. His machine was a very poor chess player and made foolish moves. After several moves the machine would be forced to give up. Today it is possible to play a fairly advanced game of chess with a computer. However, no machine has been designed that analyzes every possible strategy corresponding to any move. Even if a machine could play a million chess games a second, it would take 10^{108} years to play all the possible games.

What was the first successful **video-arcade game**?

Pong, a simple electronic version of a tennis game, was the first successful video-arcade game. Although it was first marketed in 1972, Pong was actually invented 14 years earlier in 1958 by William Higinbotham, who headed instrumentation design at Brookhaven National Laboratory at the time. Invented to amuse visitors touring the laboratory, the game was so popular that visitors would stand in line for hours to play it. Higinbotham dismantled the system two years later, and, considering it a trifle, did not patent it. In 1972, Atari released Pong, an arcade version of Higinbotham's game, and Magnavox released Odyssey, a version that could be played on home televisions.

What was the name of the **microcomputer** introduced by **Apple** in the early 1980s?

Lisa was the name of the microcomputer that Apple introduced. The forerunner of the Macintosh microcomputer, Lisa has a graphical user interface and a mouse.

What is a **silicon chip**?

A silicon chip is an almost pure piece of silicon, usually less than one centimeter square and about half a millimeter thick. It contains hundreds of thousands of microminiature electronic circuit components, mainly transistors, packed and interconnected in layers beneath the surface. These components can perform control, logic, and/or memory functions. There is a grid of thin metallic strips on the surface of the chip; these wires are used for electrical connections to other devices. The silicon chip was developed independently by two researchers: Jack Kilby of Texas Instruments in 1958, and Robert Noyce (b. 1927) of Fairchild Semiconductor in 1959.

While silicon chips are essential to most computer operation today, a myriad of other devices depend on them as well, including calculators, microwave ovens, automobile diagnostic equipment, and VCRs.

What are the **sizes of silicon chips**?

SSI—small scale integration

MSI—medium scale integration

LSI—large scale integration

VLSI—very large scale integration

ULSI—ultra large scale integration

GSI—gigascale integration

The number of components packed into a single chip is very loosely defined. ULSI units can pack millions of components on a chip. GSI, a long-term target for the industry, will potentially hold billions of components on a chip.

Are any devices being developed to **replace silicon chips**?

When transistors were introduced in 1948, they demanded less power than fragile, high-temperature vacuum tubes; allowed electronic equipment to become smaller, faster, and more dependable; and generated less heat. These developments made computers much more economical and accessible; they also made portable radios practical. However, the smaller components were harder to wire together, and hand wiring was both expensive and error-prone.

In the early 1960s, circuits on silicon chips allowed manufacturers to build increased power, speed, and memory storage into smaller packages, which required less electricity to operate and generated even less heat. While through most of the 1970s manufacturers could count on doubling the components on a chip every year without increasing the size of the chip, the size limitations of silicon chips are becoming more restrictive. Though components continue to grow smaller, the same rate of shrinking cannot be maintained.

Researchers are investigating different materials to use in making circuit chips. Gallium arsenide is harder to handle in manufacturing, but it has potential for greatly increased switching speed. Organic polymers are potentially cheaper to manufacture, and could be used for liquid-crystal and other flat screen displays, which need to have their electronic circuits spread over a wide area. Unfortunately, organic polymers do not allow electricity to pass through as well as the silicons do. Several researchers are working on hybrid chips, which could combine the benefits of organic polymers with those of silicon. Researchers are also in the initial stages of developing integrated optical chips, which would use light rather than electric current. Optical chips would generate little or no heat, would allow faster switching, and would be immune to electrical noise.

How is a **hard disk** different from a **floppy disk**?

Both types of disk use a magnetic recording surface to record, access, and erase data, in much the same way as magnetic tape records, plays, and erases sound or images. A read/write head, suspended over a spinning disk, is directed by the central processing unit (CPU) to the sector where the requested data is stored, or where the data is to be recorded. A hard disk uses rigid aluminum disks coated with iron oxide to store data. It has much greater storage capacity than several floppy disks (from 10 to hundreds of megabytes). While most hard disks used in microcomputers are "fixed" (built into the computer), some are removable. Minicomputer and mainframe hard disks include both fixed and removable hard disks (in modules called disk packs or disk cartridges). A floppy disk, also called a diskette, is made of plastic film covered with a magnetic coating, which is enclosed in a nonremovable plastic protective envelope. Floppy disks vary in storage capacity from 100 thousand bytes to more than two megabytes. Floppy disks are generally used in minicomputers and microcomputers.

In addition to storing more data, a hard disk can provide much faster access to storage than a floppy disk. A hard disk rotates from 2,400 to 3,600 revolutions per minute (rpm) and is constantly spinning (except in laptops, which conserve battery life by spinning the hard disk only when in use). An ultra-fast hard disk has a separate read/write head over each track on the disk, so that no time is lost in positioning the head over the desired track; accessing the desired sector takes only milliseconds, the time it takes for the disk to spin to the sector. A floppy disk does not spin until a data transfer is requested, and the rotation speed is only about 300 rpm.

Why does a computer **floppy disk** have to be **"formatted"**?

A disk must first be organized so that data can be stored on and retrieved from it. The data on a floppy disk or a hard disk is arranged in concentric tracks. Sectors, which can hold blocks of data, occupy arc-shaped segments of the tracks. Most floppy disks are soft-sectored, and formatting is necessary to record sector identification so that data blocks can be labeled for retrieval. Hard-sectored floppy disks use physical marks to identify sectors; these marks cannot be changed, so the disks cannot be reformatted. The way that sectors are organized and labeled dictates system compatibility: disks formatted for DOS computers can only be used in other DOS machines; those formatted for Macintoshes can only be used in other Macintoshes. Formatting erases any pre-existing data on the disk. Hard disk drives are also formatted before being initialized, and should be protected so that they are not reformatted unintentionally.

How much **data** can a **floppy disk** hold?

The three common floppy disk (diskette) sizes vary widely in storage capacity.

Envelope size (inches)	Storage capacity
8	100,000–500,000 bytes
5.25	100 kilobytes–1.2 megabytes
3.5	400 kilobytes–more than 2 megabytes

An 8-inch or 5-inch diskette is enclosed in a plastic protective envelope, which does not protect the disk from bending or folding; parts of the disk surface are also exposed, and can be contaminated by fingerprints or dust. The casing on a 3.5-inch floppy disk is rigid plastic, and includes a sliding disk guard that protects the disk surface, but allows it to be exposed when the disk is inserted in the disk drive. This protection, along with the increased data storage capacity, makes the 3.5-inch disk currently the most popular.

Who invented the computer **mouse**?

A computer "mouse" is a hand-held input device that, when rolled across a flat surface, causes a cursor to move in a corresponding way on a display screen. A prototype mouse was part of an input console demonstrated by Douglas C. Englehart in 1968 at the Fall Joint Computer Conference in San Francisco. Popularized in 1984 by the Macintosh from Apple Computer, the mouse was the result of 15 years devoted to exploring ways to make communicating with computers simpler and more flexible.

The physical appearance of the small box with the dangling, tail-like wire suggested the name of "mouse."

What is **Hopper's rule**?

Electricity travels one foot in a nanosecond (a billionth of a second). This is one of a number of rules compiled for the convenience of computer programmers. This is also considered to be a fundamental limitation on the possible speed of a computer—signals in an electrical circuit cannot move any faster.

179

Who was the first programmer?

According to historical accounts, Lord Byron's daughter, Augusta Ada Byron, the Countess of Lovelace, was the first person to write a computer program for Charles Babbage's (1792–1871) "analytical engine." This machine, never built, was to work by means of punched cards that could store partial answers that could later be retrieved for additional operations, and that would print results. Her work with Babbage and the essays she wrote about the possibilities of the "engine" established her as a "patron saint," if not a founding parent, of the art and science of programming. The programming language called "Ada" was named in her honor by the United States Department of Defense. In modern times the honor goes to Commodore Grace Murray Hopper (1906–1992) of the United States Navy. She wrote the first program for the Mark I computer.

Is an **assembly language** the same thing as a **machine language**?

While the two terms are often used interchangeably, an assembly language is a more "user friendly" translation of a machine language. A machine language is the collection of patterns of bits recognized by a central processing unit (CPU) as instructions. Each particular CPU design has its own machine language. The machine language of the CPU of a microcomputer generally includes about 75 instructions; the machine language of the CPU of a large mainframe computer may include hundreds of instructions. Each of these instructions is a pattern of 1's and 0's that tells the CPU to perform a specific operation.

An assembly language is a collection of symbolic, mnemonic names for each instruction in the machine language of its CPU. Like the machine language, the assembly language is tied to a particular CPU design. Programming in assembly language requires intimate familiarity with the CPU's architecture, and assembly language programs are difficult to maintain and require extensive documentation.

The computer language C, developed in the late 1980s, is now frequently used instead of assembly language. It is a high-level programming language that can be compiled into machine languages for almost all computers, from microcomputers to mainframes, because of its functional structure.

Who invented the **COBOL** computer language?

COBOL (common business oriented language) is a prominent computer language designed specifically for commercial uses, created in 1960 by a team drawn from several computer makers and the Pentagon. The best-known individual associated with COBOL was then-Lieutenant Grace Hopper (1906–1992) who made fundamental contributions to the United States Navy standardization of COBOL. COBOL excels at the most common kinds of data processing for business—simple arithmetic operations performed on huge files of data. The language endures because its syntax is very much like English and because a program written in COBOL for one kind of computer can run on many others without alteration.

How is a **byte** defined?

A byte, a common unit of computer storage, holds the equivalent of a single character, such as a letter (”A”), a number (”2”), a symbol (”$”), a decimal point, or a space. It is usually equivalent to eight “data bits” and one “parity bit.” A bit (a binary digit), the smallest unit of information in a digital computer, is equivalent to a single “0” or “1”. The parity bit is used to check for errors in the bits making up the byte. Although eight data bits per byte is the most common size, computer manufacturers are free to define a differing number of bits as a byte. Six data bits per byte is another common size.

What does it mean to **"boot"** a computer?

Booting a computer is starting it, in the sense of turning control over to the operating system. The term comes from bootstrap, because bootstraps allow an individual to pull on boots without help from anyone else. Some people prefer to think of the process in terms of using bootstraps to lift oneself off the ground, impossible in the physical sense, but a reasonable image for representing the process of searching for the operating system, loading it, and passing control to it. The commands to do this are embedded in a *read only memory* (ROM) chip that is automatically executed when a microcomputer is turned on or reset. In mainframe or minicomputers, the process usually involves a great deal of operator input. A *cold boot* powers on the computer and passes control to the operating system; a *warm boot* resets the operating system without powering off the computer.

Should a PC be **turned off** when not in use?

Personal computers (PCs) currently account for up to 5% of the nation's commercial energy use, and that percentage could double by the year 2000. While shutting off personal computers for one or two hours during the work day is not a cost-effective practice, turning off the monitor and leaving on the central processing unit (CPU) for the same amount of time saves a substantial fraction of the PC's energy use. However, to **181** save energy and extend the computer's lifetime, both the CPU and the monitor should be shut off at the end of the day and before the weekend.

What is the correct way to **face a computer** screen?

Correct positioning of the body at a computer is essential to preventing physical problems such as carpal tunnel syndrome and back pain. You should sit so that your eyes are 18 to 24 inches (45 to 61 centimeters) from the screen, and at a height so that they are six to eight inches (15 to 20 centimeters) above the center of the screen. Your hands should be level with or slightly below the arms.

Correct posture is also necessary. You should sit upright, keeping the spine straight. Sit all the way back in the chair with the knees level with or below the thighs. Both feet should be on the floor. The arms may rest on the desk or chair arms, but make sure you do not slouch. If you need to bend or lean forward, do so from the waist.

Where did the term **bug** originate?

The slang term *bug* is used to describe problems and errors occurring in computer programs. The term may have originated during the early 1940s at Harvard University, when computer pioneer Grace Murray Hopper discovered that a dead moth had caused the breakdown of a machine on which she was working. When asked what she was doing while removing the corpse with tweezers, she replied, "I'm debugging the machine." The moth's carcass, taped to a page of notes, is preserved with the trouble log notebook at the Virginia Naval Museum.

Grace Murray Hopper.

What is a computer **virus** and how is it spread?

Taken from the obvious analogy with biological viruses, a computer "virus" is a program that searches out other programs and "infects" them by replicating itself in them. When the programs are executed, the embedded virus is executed too, thus propagating the "infection." This normally happens invisibly to the user. A virus cannot infect other computers, however, without assistance. It is spread when users communicate by computer, often when they trade programs. The virus might do nothing but propagate itself and then allow the program to run normally. Usually, however, after propagating silently for a while, it starts doing other things—possibly inserting "cute" messages or destroying all of the user's files. Computer "worms" and "logic bombs" are similar to viruses, but they do not replicate themselves within programs as viruses do. A logic bomb does its damage immediately—destroying data, inserting garbage into data files, or reformatting the hard disk; a worm can alter the program and database either immediately or over a period of time.

In the 1990s, viruses, worms, and logic bombs have become such a serious problem, especially among IBM PC and Macintosh users, that the production of special detection and "inoculation" software has become an industry.

What is a **fuzzy search**?

Fuzzy search is a feature of some software programs that allows a user to search for text that is similar to but not exactly the same as what he or she specifies. It can produce results when the exact spelling is unknown, or it can help users obtain information that is loosely related to a topic.

What is a **pixel**?

A pixel (from the words *pix*, for picture, and *el*ement) is the smallest element on a video display screen. A screen contains thousands of pixels, each of which can be made up of one or more dots or a cluster of dots. On a simple monochrome screen, a pixel is one dot; the two colors of image and background are created when the pixel is switched either on or off. Some monochrome screen pixels can be energized to create different light intensities, to allow a range of shades from light to dark. On color screens, three dot colors are included in each pixel—red, green, and blue. The simplest screens have just one dot of each color, but more elaborate screens have pixels with clusters of each color. These more elaborate displays can show a large number of colors and intensities. On color screens, black is created by leaving all three colors off; white by all three colors on; and a range of grays by equal intensities of all the colors.

The most economical displays are monochrome, with one bit per pixel, with settings limited to on and off. High-resolution color screens, which can use a million pixels, with each color dot using four bytes of memory, would need to reserve many megabytes just to display the image.

What does **DOS** stand for?

DOS stands for "disk operating system," a program that controls the computer's transfer of data to and from a hard or floppy disk. Frequently it is combined with the main operating system. The operating system was originally developed at Seattle Computer Products as SCP-DOS. When IBM decided to build a personal computer and needed an **183** operating system, it chose the SCP-DOS after reaching an agreement with the Microsoft Corporation to produce the actual operating system. Under Microsoft, SCP-DOS became MS-DOS, which IBM referred to as PC-DOS (personal computer), and which everyone eventually simply called DOS.

What is **E mail**?

Electronic mail, also known as E mail or e-mail, uses communication facilities to transmit messages. Many systems use computers as transmitting and receiving interfaces, but fax communication is also a form of E mail. A user can send a message to a single recipient, or to many. Different systems offer different options for sending, receiving, manipulating text, and addressing. For example, a message can be "registered," so that the sender is notified when the recipient looks at the message (though there is no way to tell if the recipient has actually read the message). Many systems allow messages to be forwarded. Usually messages are stored in a simulated "mailbox" in the network server or host computer; some systems announce incoming mail if the recipient is logged onto the system. An organization (such as a corporation, university, or professional organization) can provide electronic mail facilities; national and international networks can provide them as well. In order to use E mail, both sender and receiver must have accounts on the same system or on systems connected by a network.

What is a **hacker**?

A hacker is a skilled computer user. The term originally denoted a skilled programmer, particularly one skilled in machine code and with a good knowledge of the machine and its operating system. The name arose from the fact that a good programmer could always hack an unsatisfactory system around until it worked.

The term later came to denote a user whose main interest is in defeating password systems. The term has thus acquired a pejorative sense, with the meaning of one who deliberately and sometimes criminally interferes with data available through telephone lines. The activities of such hackers have led to considerable efforts to tighten security of transmitted data.

What is a **kludge**?

A kludge (also spelled kluge) is a sloppy, crude, cumbersome solution to a problem. It refers to a makeshift solution as well as to any poorly designed product, or a product that becomes unmanageable over time.

Who coined the term **technobabble**?

John A. Barry used the term "technobabble" to mean the pervasive and indiscriminate use of computer terminology, especially as it is applied to situations that have nothing at all to do with technology. He first used it in the early 1980s.